STEPS OF BELIEF;

OR,

RATIONAL CHRISTIANITY MAINTAINED

AGAINST

ATHEISM, FREE RELIGION, AND ROMANISM.

BY

JAMES FREEMAN CLARKE.

BOSTON:
AMERICAN UNITARIAN ASSOCIATION.
1870.

WEITE Welt und breites Leben,
Langer Jahre redlich Streben,
Stets geforscht und stets gegründet,
Nie geschlossen, oft geründet,
Aeltestes bewahrt mit Treue,
Freundlich aufgefasstes Neue,
Heitern Sinn und reine Zwecke;
Nun! man kommt wohl eine Strecke.

GÖTHE.

THIRD EDITION.

CAMBRIDGE:
PRESS OF JOHN WILSON AND SON.

TO

The Memory

OF

JOHN ALBION ANDREW,

THIS BOOK IS DEDICATED.

INTRODUCTION.

THE substance of this volume was delivered last winter, to the Church of the Disciples, in Boston, as a course of Lectures. Most of it has been rewritten; but, doubtless, traces of the original form will be detected by the discerning. Such as it is, I inscribe this work with the name of one whose interest in these themes was never weakened by the cares of private business, or the responsibilities of public duty; whose insight, courage, honesty, and kindness made him dear to his friends; and whose great virtues will always illustrate the power of unsectarian and practical Christianity.

CONTENTS.

First Step.

FROM ATHEISM TO THEISM.

Second Step.

FROM THEISM TO CHRISTIANITY.

Third Step.

FROM ROMANISM TO PROTESTANTISM.

Fourth Step.

FROM THE LETTER TO THE SPIRIT.

FIRST STEP.

FROM ATHEISM TO THEISM.

"Deum sempiternum, omniscium, omnipotentem, à tergo transeuntem, vidi et obstupui."

LINNÆUS, *System of Nature.*

STEPS OF BELIEF.

CHAPTER I.

How do we know that we have a Soul; or, Materialism and Immaterialism.

ACCORDING to the oldest and most general view of human nature, man consists of two parts, — soul and body; or of three parts, — spirit, soul, and body. The soul, however, is himself: the body belongs to him. He is essentially soul: the body is his box of tools. To soul belong conscience, will, reason, love. As soul, he is free: as soul, dwelling in body, he is limited. Body helps the soul and is its servant; but, at the same time, holds it in and shuts it up. Soul aspires upward to God and heaven: body draws it down to earth and time. This has been the general belief of Chinese, Persians, Hindoos, Greeks, Romans, and Jews, — in ancient times and in modern times, — of Christians and Mohammedans, of savages and civilized, of philosopher and peasant. Almost all believe naturally that there is an immaterial principle in man, — something which cannot be seen, touched, heard, —

something not to be perceived by the senses, but only known by consciousness, — something which remains when the material envelop is dissolved and separated, which continues as a disembodied spirit when the body has returned to the elements. One proof of this wide-spread opinion is the general belief, in all ages and all lands, among the common people, of the existence of ghosts. There never has been a nation or age in which the ignorant have not believed, more or less, in the possibility of ghosts. But if there is nothing in man but body, nothing can possibly remain after the body is dissolved. If one believes, therefore, that a ghost *is possible*, though he may not believe that one ever returned, he must believe in soul. Hence it appears that a belief in soul has not prevailed among the educated and learned alone, but seems to have come to the ignorant and uneducated also, by a kind of instinct. But the wisest of our race have also believed in soul, since they have believed in a continued immortality after the dissolution of the body. Socrates and Plato — the greatest thinkers of antiquity — teach the existence of soul as independent of body, and perhaps as the source of body. The great religions of the world have taught the same, — those of ancient Egypt, Greece, Rome; those of Zoroaster, Buddha, Confucius, and Mohammed. All have agreed in the doctrine that man consists of soul as well as of body. They have taken different views of the nature of soul; but, in some sense, all have accepted it.

The body itself is something more than matter. Particles of matter, however united, do not by themselves, make a living body. Where there is life and growth, making a living body, there must be a living soul to give unity to these elements. The particles of matter in every human body come and go. We have none of the material atoms in our body to-day which we had a few years since. From whence, then, does the unity of the body come? What continually makes of these elements one and the same body? Nothing which we see, — nothing which the surgeon's knife, searching every organ, can discover, — nothing which the finest chemical analysis can detect. Yet there must be some power there, gathering, moulding, changing, distributing the carbon, oxygen, and lime; organizing them, and preserving, year after year, one and the same organic form. Compelled by these facts, Aristotle says, that, while man has a rational soul, every animal has a living soul, and every plant a vegetative soul. So the book of Genesis (in chap. I., verse 20) says, in the Hebrew, "Let the waters bring forth abundantly every moving creature that has a soul." Our translators apparently were afraid of the word, and said, "every thing that hath life." Again, in the 30th verse, the Hebrew reads: "Every beast of the field, and fowl of the air, and every thing that creepeth on the earth wherein there is a living soul." In the margin of our Bibles, the word "soul" is given for the Hebrew word. The Bible was not afraid to give a soul to animals. Whether it is an immortal soul or not, is another question. The souls of animals may be immortal. But at any rate, wherever there is life, there *must* be something more than matter, — something which no mere analysis of matter can reach.

The language of Jesus asserts the reality of the soul, and its continued existence after death. He says, "Be not afraid of them that kill the body, and after that have no more that they can do. But I will forewarn you whom ye shall fear: Fear him, which after he hath killed, hath power to cast into hell; yea, I say unto you, fear him." The apostle speaks of "fleshly lusts which war against the soul." Christ is called "the Shepherd of souls." We are told "to possess our souls in patience," and to "purify our souls by obeying the truth." Finally, Paul prays that our whole "spirit, soul, and body may be kept blameless." He also makes a distinction between this present body — the life of which comes from the soul — and the future body, which shall be spiritual; that is, moulded by, and subject to, the highest principle in man. Man is a soul, according to the New Testament. His identity and personality are in his soul. His soul may be drawn down by his body, and become a carnal or merely animal soul; or it may be raised up by the spiritual part into communion with God, devotion to eternal truth, obedience to duty, and be inspired through and through by faith, hope, and love. Then it becomes a spiritual soul. Just so, the body may be so depraved and stupefied as to have only a sort of vegetable life, and the soul then becomes a kind of vegetable soul; or it may be raised up until it becomes a spiritual body, such as we hope to have in the other world. Such also we have seen glimpses of in this world. In the great inspired moments of life, the spiritual body shines out even here; as it did when they looked at Stephen, and "saw his face as it had been the face of an angel."

I do not quote these passages from the New Testament as proofs of the existence of the soul. I only refer to them as part of the history of opinion, to illustrate the universal belief in an immaterial principle which informs and vitalizes the body. The most obvious proof of its existence, and that which has probably produced this wide-spread belief in the soul, is the unity of all organized and living beings. In such beings, all the parts are correlated, to use an expression taken from Kant. This philosopher says, that, in a living body, the cause of the mode of existence of each part is contained in the whole. Death leaves each part free to pass through changes belonging to itself alone. Cuvier gives a similar definition of the living body. Every organized being, he says, forms a whole; a close corporation in which every part acts in relation to the action of the whole. All its organs are correlated to each other. If it is a carnivorous animal, its teeth, its claws, its organs of motion, its senses, its digestive organs, are adapted to this end. A living body grows, not by juxtaposition (as is the case with a stone), but by intra-susception, or growth from within. Life is a power which resists chemical laws, which begin to take effect on the body as soon as death arrives. Even if life has a physical basis, in a peculiarly organized substance, this does not explain the *unity* of a living body. What carries on that which may be called "the vital vortex," or perpetual exchange of particles; the old being taken away, and new ones put in their place? There is a unity to every organized and living body, which is not in the separate parts, nor in the separate parts taken together. It is nothing which the senses can perceive, which chemistry can detect, — nothing possessing material properties. Then it is not any thing material.

It may be said that we find occasionally an apparent unity in a physical body, in which the particles come and go, but the same form remains; and yet where no one suspects the existence of a soul. For example, a cloud sometimes remains stationary over the top of a mountain, preserving the same form, while all the particles of aqueous vapor of which it is composed are rushing into it on one side, and out of it on the other. So, there are found on the surface of a glacier, deep wells called *moulins*, which always keep the same position, though the particles of ice are moving steadily on, day by day, at the rate of one or two feet every twenty-four hours. But in these cases the unity comes from external physical forces, which can be observed. When the aqueous vapor, in an invisible state, is carried by the wind against the side of the mountain, it is obliged to rise in order to pass over it. When it reaches a certain height, the temperature is such that it is precipitated, and becomes visible. Passing on, it crosses the summit, descends on the other side, and arrives at a higher temperature as it descends the mountain side, which causes it to evaporate, or become invisible. External forces produce these results. But no external forces create or preserve the unity of the living body. That is something acting on it from within; and this something escapes all the tests which detect physical facts and laws.

Nevertheless, there has almost always been a minority which has taken a different view, and declared that there was nothing in man but matter, and the results of matter. The Sadducees among the Jews, the Epicureans among the Greeks and Romans, the Materialists in modern times, have so thought. They argue in this way; "We are certain of the existence of matter, but not certain of the existence of any thing else. We know that we have a body: we do not know that we have a soul. The existence of soul is therefore an hypothesis; and an unnecessary one, because all mental phenomena may be accounted for, as resulting from matter. If body can separate blood into bone and muscle; if it can digest food, and make chemical compounds of the air, — why can it not also produce thought and feeling? If the liver can secrete bile, why may not the brain secrete ideas? Till we find out all that body can do, and reach its limit, why think that there is any thing more? Let us be contented with one cause until more are found to be necessary."

Certain facts of experience seem also to confirm the views of Materialists. For example, when the body is well and strong, the thoughts and feelings are also sound and healthy; when the body is sick and weak, the mind is weakened too. When the body grows old and feeble, the memory is impaired, the judgment is less vigorous, the feelings grow torpid. When the body dies, there is nothing more seen or known of the man. "As far as we know, the man has also come to an end," says the Materialist; denying, of course, all the accounts of spiritual appearances. A stone falls on your head, and a little bit of the skull presses on the brain. All thought immediately stops, and remains suspended, until the surgeon comes and trepans the skull, and removes the pressure. Instantly thought, feeling, will return. "Does not this show that the soul is the result of the body?" asks the Materialist.

"By no means," replies the Immaterialist. "It only proves, that, while the soul is connected with the body, it cannot do its work without it.. Deprive a skilful carpenter of his tool-chest, and he becomes helpless: he can do nothing. Does that prove that the carpenter is the result of his tool-chest? The body is the tool-chest which the soul uses; it is helpless without it: but it does not follow from that that the soul is the result of the body. That the soul, in this world, can do nothing without its body, no more proves that the soul comes from the body, than the fact that a surgeon cannot operate without his instruments, proves the surgeon to be the result and growth of his instruments. The soul is in full activity, — thinking, feeling, acting. An extra drop of blood in the brain stops all this thought in a moment. True. And so, an astronomer is making some great discovery through his telescope. A film of mist comes over the object-glass. His discovery stops in a moment: all his power comes to an end. But you would not say that the astronomer was the result of the telescope, because he cannot act without his telescope. Why, then, argue that the soul is the result of body, because it cannot act without the the body? *

* It has been said that these analogies are inadequate, because we know the existence of the carpenter and surgeon, but do not know the existence of soul. If the object of my illustration was to *prove* the existence of soul, the objection would be valid. But it is not: it is to answer the objection to its existence drawn from the facts which show the dependence of soul on body. The Materialist argues that because the phenomena of thought, &c., *depend* on the condition of the body, they must be the result of body. I reply that this is not necessary, because, in other instances, certain manifestations depend on the condition of certain bodies; but we know that they do not result from them. If you say that A can never appear except under certain conditions of B, and therefore A is a result or a property of B, I may answer you by showing that C never appears except under certain conditions of D, and yet it is certain that C is not the result of D.

The soul is like a musician sitting at his organ, and drawing from it delicate and delicious music. But the instrument grows old, — the bellows refuse to supply the air to the pipes; the pipes crack; the keys are out of joint. The musician no longer can play as before. As the organ gradually grows old, weak, dilapidated, out of tune, the power of the musician seems to grow weak too. At last the organ refuses to give a sound. It stops. The musical power stops too, at the same time. Do you infer from that, that the musician is dead, or that he is only a property of the organ? No. Give him a new instrument, and you will see that his power is as great as ever. So, when the human body grows old, the brain becomes feeble: and we cannot recollect as we once could; we cannot think as we once could. That is because the instrument of thought, love, memory, and imagination has decayed: that is all. Give the soul a new instrument, a spiritual body; and it will be seen that its power is the same as ever.

The Materialist says, "We are certain of the existence of matter, not of spirit. We know that we have a body: we do not know that we have a soul." I deny the fact. I assert that we are no more certain of the existence of body, than we are of the existence of soul. All we know of body is its properties, — that it is hard or soft, square or round, sweet or bitter, colored or colorless, fragrant or inodorous, having taste or insipid. Just so we know the qualities of soul, —

that it is something which thinks, remembers, hopes, fears, loves and hates, chooses and refuses. I am just as certain that I love, that I think, that I choose, — as I am that I can touch, taste, and smell. I know my thought as certainly as I know my sensations.

You say, we know what matter is, but do not know what soul is. What, then, is matter? All you can say is, *that which we perceive through the senses*, that is matter. Matter is that which I can see with my eyes, taste with my tongue, touch with my hands, smell with my nose, hear with my ears. Very well. But I cannot touch a thought, or taste a feeling, or smell a resolution, or measure the size of my hope and fear. Then these are not matter, but something else. Then there is something else in the world besides matter; and something of whose existence we are just as certain as we are of the existence of matter.

But we must go further. I am more certain of soul than I am of body. Let me suppose that I have some bodily substance before me, — say an apple. I perceive the apple; but what do I perceive? I perceive, you say, something round, colored, fragrant, and with taste. By no means. What I perceive is the sensation in myself of roundness, of color, of fragrance. But the sensation is in my mind. How do I know that there is something round and red and sweet outside of my organs of taste and smell and touch? All I perceive is the sensation. But the sensation is not in the apple, is it? the sensation is in myself. How do I know that there is an apple outside of myself, — outside of my sensation? I admit that I do know it; but how do I know it? I answer that I *infer* it, by an act of reason. I reason spontaneously and instinctively that there must be something outside of me to give me these sensations, because I cannot create them in myself when I choose. So I call that which acts upon me, through my senses, matter. But the sensation, which is in my mind and is immaterial, is more certain than the inference from the sensation. I know the sensation: I infer the existence of the apple.

No doubt, in all this, the mind acts irresistibly and necessarily. When we perceive outward phenomena, through the senses, we are obliged to infer that there is some substance in which they inhere. We call that substance matter. Exactly in the same way, when we perceive inward phenomena through consciousness; when we perceive in ourselves thoughts and feelings, — we are obliged, by a law of our nature, to infer that there is substance in which they inhere, and we call it soul or spirit. And as all the phenomena or qualities of body are different from those of mind, and as all we know of substances is through their phenomena, we are obliged to infer that the substances are different; that is, that there are two substances, — body and soul.

Therefore, whenever any one asks me, "How do you know that there is such a fact as soul?" I may immediately reply, "How do you know that there is such a fact as body? Tell me that, and I will tell you how I know that there is soul." All that you know of body are its qualities, properties, or phenomena; these qualities are all sensible qualities, perceived through the senses. As these qualities are all linked together and co-ordinated, you are obliged to suppose something which unites them, and you call that something matter. Exactly in the same way, all I know of mind are its qualities, properties, or phenomena; and I know all of these through my consciousness. I do not see, smell, or taste my thoughts; but I am conscious of my thoughts. And as my thoughts and feelings and will are all united together and co-ordinated, I am obliged to suppose something which unites them, and I call that something mind or soul or spirit.

We see, therefore, that we are just as sure of the existence of the soul, as we are of the existence of the body; and that no possible proof can be given of the reality of the outward world, which cannot also be given of the real existence of the soul. And I do not think there is a child, capable of understanding any thing, who may not understand this. But I wish to make it a little plainer still.

If the conditions of the body affect the soul, the conditions of the soul also affect the body. A man is in perfect bodily health. A letter is brought to him. He opens it, reads it, and instantly faints away, falling on the ground as if dead. The thought communicated to the mind has acted instantly on the body, causing a reverse action of the heart, and drawing the blood from the brain. No physical cause can account for this result. Nothing has happened to his body, except what came to it from the mind. Again, something is said on the other side of the room, and it makes you blush; that is, the thought communicated to your soul acts on the blood, and causes it to mount into the capillaries of the face. The soul acts on the body as often as the body acts on the soul. Now if, because the condition of the body affects the mind, you argue that the mind is material, — then, when the condition of the mind affects the body, you ought to argue that the body is immaterial. If one class of facts proves the soul to be a property of the body, the other class of facts proves the body to be a property of the soul. Accordingly, many persons do argue that there is only one substance; but that this is not matter, but spirit. This theory, which makes every thing spirit, is certainly more reasonable than that which makes every thing matter. But neither is borne out by facts. The facts go to show that there are two substances, — soul and body; and that man is a soul, dwelling at present in a body, which is the garment he wears, the house he lives in, but which he is to lay aside for a house not made with hands, for a heavenly garment to be worn hereafter.*

* It may be said that, while Materialism assumes that there is only one substance, namely, matter; and while Spiritualism also assumes only one substance, namely, spirit, —

We are conscious of ourselves as units; and there is no higher evidence than consciousness. Matter is divisible and extended: every material substance may be conceived of as having parts, — upper and lower, inward and outward, right side and left side. But we cannot conceive of ourselves in this way. We say "*I* think, *I* feel, *I* wish, *I* dislike;" but we cannot conceive of this "*I*," which loves and hates, as being long or short, divisible, extended, having an upper and under side to it. Therefore, the "*I*" of which we are conscious is not a material but an immaterial substance; since it does not possess the properties essential to all matter, which are extension and divisibility.

As long as the mind is united with the body, the condition of the body affects it. We are comfortable

---

there is a third alternative better still. This is to assume one substance which manifests itself indifferently as either matter or spirit, — the mysterious substratum, fountain, or cause from which both proceed. No doubt God is one; and in him is to be found the source of matter as well as of spirit. They have their unity in him. To suppose otherwise, to treat matter as an outlying substance, alien from God, a dark material to be worked upon by his power, is to fall into a false dualism. I grant this. But that must often be distinguished which cannot be divided. The human soul, no less than matter, must rest ultimately in God. Neither is *that* an outlying substance, independent of him. He is a perpetual creator both of matter and souls. Still, we must no more confound body with soul, than we must confound soul with God. The distinction of matter and spirit is as important as their unity; and, without the previous analysis, the ultimate synthesis is impossible.

or uncomfortable, according as the house we live in is comfortable or uncomfortable. But if mind were the result of body, as music is the result of a musical-box, then the condition of the body would always and regularly influence the mind. In that case, given the condition of the body, and you could always infer the condition of the soul. When I know the condition of the barrel, pins, and springs in the box, I can always tell what kind of music it will make. But this is not the case with the nature of man. Let the soul be inspired with profound convictions, by living ideas, by large affections, and it rises superior to its body: it "o'erinforms its tenement of clay." The wife and mother, feeble before, become strong and enduring, when they are called on to nurse a husband or a child. The soul compels the body to serve it, and do its will; gives it a strength not its own; enables it to bear long fatigue, watching, want of sleep, want of food; reverses all the common hygienic laws. How often a great mental excitement will at once cure a bodily disease! One of these days we shall probably have a mind-cure; and then we shall send sick people to establishments where the body will be cured by well-arranged and properly administered mental stimulants and mental food. People will be talked into health, sung into health; and the wise physician, instead of potions and pills, will prescribe great thoughts and beautiful ideas. I have known instances of persons given over by their physicians, who saved their lives by resolving not to die, putting forth such a vigor of will as conquered and drove back the creeping approach of death. The mind sometimes grows young, as the body grows old. As the poor house of clay wears to pieces, the soul within spires upward in an increasing flame of light and love. The body decays, but the soul continues to go onward and upward, onward and upward, till the body drops from it, and leaves it more alive than ever.

If the health of the soul depends on that of the body, — as we are in the habit of saying so frequently, — it is no less true that bodily health depends very much on mental health. A conscience at ease; a mind which trusts in Providence and is not anxious; a heart which does not devour itself with jealousy, envy, and hatred, but has a joyful sympathy with all around, — these keep the body well and young. Fear, anxiety, gloom, bad-temper, make us prematurely old. If we wish to be in good health, we ought, indeed, to have well-ventilated apartments, to take enough exercise, be careful of what we eat and drink; but chiefly we must have courage, faith, hope, and love.

Perhaps you will say, "What is the use of all this argument? Man is the same being, whatever theory we take of his substance, — whether we call it matter, or call it spirit." But this is no mere question of words. It is a question whether we shall look down or look up. Whatever we believe ourselves to be, we are likely to endeavor to do. If we say, "Man is only a higher animal; he grows as a vegetable grows, — by force of the root and stalk, sun and rain; he is made to eat and drink; digest; inhale and exhale the air; obey his appetites; gratify his passions; then grow old, and fade away," — if we say this and believe this of ourselves, we shall *do* this and no more. But if we believe there is something within us which can react on matter; which can control and conquer the appetites and senses; which can soar upward to the seventh heaven of thought and love; which can live according to conscience and reason; which can adopt a plan, and adhere to it, — then we shall be more likely to live that way, and become what we believe ourselves capable of becoming.

I reverence the magnificence of nature, and see God present in it. Often, on a winter's night, when the sky is sparkling with innumerable stars, I have gone out and looked hour after hour through my telescope at the majestic orbs, — the great double-stars, blue and yellow, orange and purple; the clustering brilliant constellations, blazing like a crown of diamonds in the sky, — and have at last felt almost as if I had left this little planet, and was roaming through the infinite universe of God. I love the majesty of the mountains, rising in solemn grandeur into the silent circumambient air; great sentinels, keeping watch for thousands of years above the homes of men. I can sit all day watching the ocean, as it rolls, in never-ending harmonies of sound, its incessant waves. I am at home in the peaceful woods, when the flickering light falls amid the numerous leaves, and every plant and bush has a beauty all its own. But what are all these to the soul of man, — to the majestic intellect which can mete out the heavens with a span, and comprehend the dust of the earth in a measure, and weigh the mountains in scales? What is the glory of the midnight heavens to that of a great spirit which rises to truth and God, and lifts up nations with it, — the soul of a Zoroaster or a Confucius, of a Socrates or a Paul? Such souls break the chains of sense and selfishness for millions, and make mankind free to follow the truth. "The glory of the terrestrial is one: the glory of the celestial is another." What is the exquisite beauty of a flower to the tender motherly love which beams on the little infant, and radiates light and life into its breast?

A young man, nursed in affection; lapped in luxury; fed on literature, art, and science; just entering life, which opens its hospitable arms to welcome him to fame, influence, and love, — hears the cry of his country in her hour of danger, renounces all his cherished hopes at that solemn call, and goes to die, torn by shot and shell, amid the rage and curses of foes. So young Shaw died on the parapets of Wagner, and a thousand others elsewhere. And while I marvel at this power of spirit, my Materialist comes, and says, "Oh! it was the action of some of the lobes of the brain. The gray matter of the nervous tissue secreted patriotism and conscience, as the liver secretes bile." I cannot believe him. "That which is born of flesh is flesh, but that which is born of spirit is spirit."

More than twenty-three centuries have passed since the son of Sophroniscus taught in the streets of Athens. He might have lived a comfortable life; he might have used his wonderful intellect in getting riches or power, and died among troops of friends. No: he devoted himself to teaching the young men to be just, to be generous, to be lovers of truth and beauty, above all else. He taught the grandeur of the soul; taught that the body was not the man, but the soul was the man; denounced all meanness; made enemies of the powerful; and, at last, when condemned to die, spent a summer's day in discoursing on immortality with his disciples. At the close of the conversation, when he was about to drink the hemlock, one of his disciples asked him how he wished to be buried. "Any way you please," he replied, "if you can catch me to bury me. You seem to think, after all I have said, that this body is Socrates." The Materialist thinks so still, and considers that wonderful truth, which uplifts us and teaches us across all these centuries, was only the secretion of a little gray pulp in the brain.

Body, make what you will of it, be it ever so subtle and ethereal, can never be refined into soul. Body is composed of parts, infinitely divisible; soul is a unit, incapable of division. If I am only body, then at death, when the body is dissolved, I am dissolved; I pass into the life of nature; I become a part of earth and air and water. Faith in immortality disappears with this doctrine.

I stand by the grave of a friend, a dear and noble character, one whom I love better than myself. I have seen him growing from good to better. I have seen him conquering his passions; curbing his self-will; accepting the great law of duty as the rule of his life; trusting absolutely in God's providence amid all disaster, disappointment, failure. I have seen him thus going forward, ever forward; becoming more simple, more tender, more exquisitely conscious of God's love, from year to year. His presence was a blessing wherever he passed. His words dropped from his lips freighted with generous influence. You went from him better and happier. At last, in his prime, in the midst of his great usefulness, he falls. I come and look on that pale forehead for the last time. I say: "We only seem the dead, who stay behind: he has gone into fuller life." "Pshaw!" says the Materialist, "that is very unscientific. He has become carbon and hydrogen. He was only organized matter: now he is disorganized and dissolved. Some one else will take his place in the universe; but he is gone for ever."

Of course, I do not say that all Materialists deny a hereafter. But this is the natural tendency of Materialism. Materialism naturally tends to deny any future life. To realize immortality, we must believe in a soul, which is our real self; which is a unit, indivisible and indestructible; which gives unity to the body while it is in it, and organizes continually all particles of matter according to its own type. We must believe in a soul which is also capable of organizing ideas and thoughts; capable of free movement; capable of deliberately choosing an end, according to reason, and then going forward to it. We must believe in a soul, not the creature, but the creator, of circumstances, with inexhaustible capacities of knowledge and love. Only thus can we realize immortality.

But Materialism does more than this: it takes away God.

If all that we know is matter, — if all that we call thought is the result of matter, — then we know nothing, and can know nothing, of God, the infinite Spirit. According to Materialism, matter develops itself by laws of its own into mineral, vegetable, and animal life; and then evolves out of these what we call thought, love, and will. Man is not created; he is evolved: the world is not created; it develops itself. God is dethroned by Materialism; and another deity, the Law of Development, is placed in the temple to be worshipped in his place.

The foundation of our knowledge of God is what we learn of spirit in ourselves. We call God the infinite Mind, adding the conception of the infinite to the consciousness of our own reason. We call him supreme goodness, holiness, freedom; but to attach any meaning to these terms, we must study them in ourselves. If we consider all that is spiritual in ourselves to be only highly developed matter, then we shall be unable to believe in any other God than the universe itself. The universe, then, is self-created; it has no Creator: it is self-governed; it has no Ruler: it rolls on its dark path to no foreseen and prepared end, but only as blind chance and iron fate may determine. Materialism, carried out logically, ends in atheism.

But, fortunately, man was not made to be satisfied with this barren doctrine. He was made to believe in soul as well as body, in unity no less than in variety, in freedom as well as in law, in spirit as much as in matter, in an immortal future as in a mortal present, in God as in the world. Science means knowledge; and we *know* soul, God, and eternity just as well, and in exactly the same way, as we know body, the world, and time. Only let us cherish this higher knowledge. Let us understand that our dignity, our freedom, our nobleness, consist in looking at the spiritual and immortal side of our being, and rising evermore above time and sense to that which transcends time and sense, and remains when these leave us for ever, when time shall be no longer, and the heavens shall depart as a scroll that is rolled together. For such shall soul be, even if all matter disappears and comes to an end.*

---

* It is sometimes said, that it is improper to argue from the bad consequences of any theory to its untruth; and it may be urged that I do this in the latter part of this chapter. I do

NOTE.

The scientific Materialism, so called, of the present day comes from Germany, and seems a reaction against the extreme idealism of Fichte, Schelling, and Hegel. The chief representative of this school of Materialism is Büchner, author of the book called "Force and Matter" (*Kraft und Stoff*). In this book, Materialism finds a sort of pocket-manual. Its fundamental principle is this: "There is no force without matter: there is no matter without force." The theory is, that force is a property of matter; and matter therefore remains the only substance. Both matter and force have always existed, and existed together. It is absurd to conceive of a force outside of matter, or above it. Life is developed by spontaneous generation from the lowest germ; and, by transformation of species, man at last arrives. Of course, thought

---

indeed endeavor to show that Materialism tends to destroy the generous and noble sentiments of the soul, to weaken our faith in God, to quench our hope of immortality. But is this an *argumentum ad invidiam?* If I can prove that a certain belief A, is inconsistent with other beliefs B, C, D, of which other beliefs we have good evidence, is not that, so far, a reason for rejecting the belief A?

When Paul was contending against the general proposition of certain Corinthians, — viz., that "there is no resurrection of the dead," — he argued from the consequences of this proposition. "If there be no resurrection of the dead, then is Christ not risen. And if Christ be not risen, then is our preaching vain, and your faith also is vain," &c. Is this an *argumentum ad invidiam?* No. Paul simply said, "If you accept this proposition, you will be obliged, logically, to reject other beliefs which you have already received on good evidence. If you have accepted those other propositions on good grounds, then so far you have good grounds for rejecting this."

and will are products of matter. Moleschott says, "Without phosphorus, no thought," a proposition which the Spiritualist will not care to deny. But he also adds, "Thcught is a movement of matter," a proposition much more doubtful. Büchner's work is written with power and clearness, and has passed through many editions in England, France, and Germany. He does not take the trouble to give a definition of matter, but believes it to be infinitely divisible, in opposition to the atomic theory. This gives M. Paul Janet,* one of his critics, occasion to remark that the very conception of matter disappears if you conceive it to be infinitely divisible. For, says he, if we imagine a heap of sand, the only reality in it consists in the particles of sand of which it is composed. Their composition in a heap is only the sum of these particles, and is purely form, not substance. Now, take one of these particles, and suppose it to be divided

---

It shows a *want* of intellectual acumen to accept a proposition on the basis of a certain argument, without first looking to see whether it is coherent or incoherent with other propositions which are already a part of our intellectual system of thought.

Wrong to look at consequences! Does not the man of science look at consequences before accepting any new theory in chemistry, geology, or astronomy? He says, "How is this to be reconciled with what we know already? Is this consistent or otherwise with the ascertained facts and laws of science?" It would be childish not to put this test to every hypothesis which asserts itself as truth. All truth is consistent with itself; and it is a sufficient argument against any theory, that it calls upon us to reject what we have already found to be true. That the tree is known by its fruits is not yet a wholly antiquated maxim.

* *Le Matérialisme Contemporaine*, par Paul Janet. 1864.

into a million parts, — the only reality will then consist in the parts, and not in their composition. But each of these parts is again divisible, and so the reality departs from it again into the particles into which it is divided. Go on for ever in this operation, and the reality perpetually disappears and becomes something relative and provisional. It is not in the form or heap, nor in the particles. It must, then, be subject to some condition outside of itself. But this unknown condition or principle, not being material, must be immaterial. Consequently, Büchner's doctrine of the infinite divisibility of matter, leads through Materialism back to Idealism.

M. Büchner's critics find him equally weak when he considers the relation of matter to motion. They use against him the scientific doctrine of *inertia*, accepted by most philosophers, from Newton to Laplace. This doctrine is that of the indifference of matter as respects motion or rest. If put in motion, it has no tendency to stop; if at rest, no tendency to move. This is a fundamental law of science, without which some sciences, astronomy for example, would be impossible; for this tendency in matter to motion or rest would enter as an unknown element into every calculation and derange its results. Every astronomical verification, therefore, is a proof of the doctrine of *inertia*, and so disproves the statement that force is a property of matter. Force must be something outside of matter, and is admitted (says Mr. Martineau) both by Comte and Mill to be hyperphysical. Mr. Martineau very clearly shows (in his article on "Nature and God"), that all force is of one type, and that type mind. Thus we have another confutation of Materialism, derived from one of the fundamental laws of physical science.

CHAPTER II.

WHY DO WE BELIEVE IN GOD? OR, THE EVIDENCES OF THEISM.

THE present chapter has two subjects: first, Why do we believe in God? second, What are the proofs of His existence?

These two questions are very different ones, and may require very different answers. It is one thing to believe a fact, another thing to prove it. A proof is only one kind of evidence: it is evidence addressed to the logical understanding. But we believe a great many facts, which we have never had proved to us, and which we cannot prove to others. I believe my own existence. I not only believe it, but I know it. This is the most certain knowledge we have; for if we doubt our own existence, the very doubt is evidence that we exist. We could not doubt, unless we existed to doubt. We are so certain of our existence, that we cannot disbelieve it, if we try to do so. And yet, though we know our own existence as an absolute certainty, we cannot prove it logically, in any way, to a disbeliever. Suppose I should say: "Prove that you exist. I deny your existence; now prove it."

You reply perhaps: "You see me, you hear me speak, I touch you with my hand; that is proof." "No," I answer: "I seem to see you, I fancy that I hear you speak, I appear to touch you with my hand. But in dreams I see and hear people; and they talk to me, and tell me what I did not know before. They seem as real as you do. How do I know that I am not dreaming about you? Prove to me that you are a substance outside of my mind, and not such substances as dreams are made of." You cannot do it. No man can do it. No one can prove his own existence to another, nor to himself. He is conscious of his own existence, and so he knows it; that is all, but that is enough.

In the same way, it is impossible to prove to a doubter the existence of an outside world. If I doubt the existence of an outside world, you cannot prove it to me by any argument or chain of logic. You say to me: "Do not you see it? do not you touch it? does it not seem outside of yourself?" "Certainly," I reply, "it seems outside of myself; and so do the images in my dreams seem outside of myself. I am only aware of my own sensations: how do I know that there is any thing real corresponding to them outside of me?" You cannot get beyond this. If a man is not satisfied with the evidence of consciousness, and wishes a logical proof addressed to his understanding of the existence of an outside world, he cannot have it. We can neither prove our own existence nor that of the world, to one who questions the evidence of consciousness. The two facts of which all mankind are certain are incapable of proof.

And, if we could prove the existence of the outside world by means of logical arguments, we should not make it more certain, but less so. We should bring it down from the sphere of knowledge to that of probability. An argument can only produce probability. It can produce a very strong degree of belief, — a belief so strong as to be almost as good as certainty for all practical purposes; but it is not so certain as experience. We believe, on the ground of argument, that there is such a place as London, or that there was such a man as Julius Cæsar; and our belief is almost equal to certainty, but not quite. If we had talked with Julius Cæsar, if we had lived in London, we should have been more certain. Intuition and experience give a higher certainty than argument can produce.

If a man has no ear for music, and does not know the difference between two tunes, you may convince him by argument that there is such a thing as music. You can say: "If music does not exist, is it likely that men and women should spend so much time and money in concerts, oratorios, and in taking musical lessons; that they should make and buy pianos, flutes, violins, trumpets, harps, and organs; that in all lands and all times there should have been musical instruments, tunes, and songs? Is it probable that mankind should have entered into this great conspiracy among themselves to impose on each other? Is it not more probable that music is a reality?" And the man, very likely, would be entirely convinced by this argument. But his belief in music, based on such an argument, must evidently be very much less strong, than if he himself had a sense of melody, harmony, tune, and time, and thereby knew the reality of music.

Just so, you can convince a man born blind, by dint of argument, that there is a visible world of color and grace, of light and shade. Since all men, except a very few, agree in this, you may argue that it is more likely that the few should be deficient in the sense of sight, than that the many should be mistaken in thinking that they see. Since, in all lands and all times men have agreed in speaking of a visible universe, it may be highly probable even to a blind man that there is such a universe. But if he could *see* it, this probability would at once rise into knowledge.

In the same way, we can adduce evidence which ought to convince the atheist, of the very high probability of God's existence. Perhaps, as some men are color-blind and others are music-deaf, there may be some persons blind and deaf toward God, whose spiritual senses are dull and as yet undeveloped. We may give such persons very good reasons for believing, on grounds of argument, that God exists. Such reasons I will now proceed to give. But I wish it to be understood that I am only attempting to make the existence of God probable by means of proofs: by and by, I shall show how it is that we can know God, by a certainty above all argument, higher than all logic, and more satisfactory than any process of reasoning ever can be.

And, first, we may say to our atheist, — just as we would say to our deaf man, or our blind man, — "Is it probable that men, in all lands and times, should enter into a conspiracy to make believe that there is a God? Differing from each other in all possible ways as to what sort of a being God is; fighting together and murdering each other, about these differences, — the vast majority of mankind, in all ages, have yet believed in Beings, or a Being, above this world, and higher than man, — the Maker, Ruler, Law-giver of this universe. Is this universal faith likely to be an invention or a deception? Is it a tree without a root? Is it an effect without a cause? Is it not far more likely that man is naturally a religious being, that he has an organ by which he can perceive the infinite, the eternal, the supernatural, as a reality? Unless there is a supernatural world, unless there is a God, — a God whom men perceive, faintly or clearly, — how can you account for this universal faith of the human race in the supernatural world and in God?"

The atheistic answer to this argument sometimes is, that religion is the work of priests, who have invented it, and who keep it up as a cheat, in order to get a support out of men, by playing on their credulity and their fear. You may weigh the force of this answer by observing how it would sound in another case. Suppose the man who had no ear for music should say, "Oh yes! I know that men have always had what they called music; but this has been an invention of the musicians. They have imposed on men by making them believe there was such a thing as music, merely to get a support out of them by selling their organs and pianos. Music results from a conspiracy of the musical-instrument makers and musicians."

A proof of the existence of God — usually called the ontological proof — is to be found in the very idea of God existing in the human mind. How did man get the idea of an infinite and perfect Being? He does not find any thing in himself infinite and perfect: he is finite and imperfect. He does not find any thing outside of himself infinite or perfect. The world of nature is, as far as his organs of observation reach, finite and imperfect. Did he invent this notion of an infinite and perfect Being? But then he must have invented it out of nothing; for there is nothing similar to it in the universe. All that we perceive outside of ourselves, all that we feel within ourselves, is finite. Yet we all have a clear conception of an infinite, supreme, and perfect Being. Is it not probable that this idea comes to us by means of a spiritual organ, the object of which is the infinite and perfect Being? If we did not find this idea in ourselves, if we did not find it in the outward world, if we could not have created it out of nothing, — how did we get it, except by receiving it through our spiritual nature, or our higher reason, — that is, by seeing the infinite and perfect Being, through the eye of the soul? An argument something like this has seemed satisfactory to some of the greatest minds the world has produced. It has been declared a complete proof of the existence of God, by Anselm, Descartes, Spinoza, Leibnitz. "For," say they, "we have the idea of a perfect Being in our minds. But existence is a part of this idea, and a necessary part; for an imaginary being is less perfect than a real being. Therefore, we are so made as necessarily to believe in the existence of a perfect Being. Whenever we think of God, we are obliged to think of him as existing. And we can have no higher proof of any reality, than that we necessarily believe in its existence, so soon as the idea of it arises in our mind."

I showed in the first chapter why it is that we believe in the soul as a real substance. I said that we believe in the soul for the same reason that we believe in body or matter. All that we perceive of matter are its phenomena, which are known to us through the senses; and we find all these sensible phenomena going together, or correlated: hence we infer one substance in which they inhere and call it matter. Just so we said, all that we perceive of mind are its phenomena, which are known to us through consciousness. We are conscious of thought, feeling, hope, fear, will, effect; and we find them all also correlated, — all belong together; hence we infer a substance in which they inhere, and call it soul. But, now, all these phenomena are finite, changing, limited, imperfect. Yet there are also certain infinite phenomena. We perceive certain phenomena as infinite. We cannot limit space or time; we cannot limit power or cause; we cannot limit truth or goodness. Above all finite powers and causes, above all finite laws, above all finite goodness, we perceive infinite power, infinite wisdom, infinite goodness. And as all these are correlated and go together, we infer substance in which they all inhere, and call it God. Just as we infer matter, as the necessary basis of sensible phenomena, we infer God as the necessary basis of spiritual phenomena; and this by a spontaneous act of the reason in all these three cases. We infer matter from material phenomena; we infer mind from mental phenomena; and we infer God from spiritual phenomena.

Then, after the ontological argument for the existence of God, comes what is called the cosmological argument.

Where did the world come from? It did not make itself; and we did not make it. The modern answer of some philosophers seems to be stolen from Topsy. Topsy says, "I wasn't made, Missis: 'spects I growed." So these philosophers say, "The world grew: it was developed." But let us not be cheated by words. An advancing world needs an author, quite as much as a world which stands still. A world which has the power of unfolding itself out of chaos into perfect order and beauty, demands a cause, even more than an unchanging world.

Every thing we perceive in the outward universe is dependent. The mineral kingdom is held fast by gravitation to its place, and is moved to and fro by force outside of itself. The vegetable kingdom depends on earth, air, water, for its life. The animal kingdom depends on the vegetable kingdom and the mineral. And the earth itself, with all on it, depends on the sun for motion, light, heat, growth, life. These all depend on each other: none can stand alone or go alone.* But on what do all depend? Whence comes the order, the arrangement, the growth, the permanence of them all, fusing them into a whole, a Kosmos of order and beauty? Every thing that we see, hear, and know in the outward universe is dependent: on what do all depend? What hand holds them all up? What mind plans, every day, the events which are to happen in the universe? This great world is only as a little infant which cannot take a single step alone. What parent watches its tottering footsteps, and makes provision for its ignorant future?

Development is a word very easy to say. But the

---

* Recent physical researches in solar astronomy show that the sun depends on the planets, and is very sensitive to their influence.

history of this earth shows crisis as well as development. I go out with my geological teacher for a ramble. He shows me, under my feet, the traces of awful convulsions, of times when the solid rocks rolled in liquid fire; when the atmosphere, a hundred miles high, was filled with gases no animal lungs could breathe. He shows me other long periods in which an immeasurable ocean rolled above our continents, depositing them in successive strata, through uncalculated myriads of years. Again, he shows me other epochs during which fearful animals crawled amid the slime of a half-dried earth, and devoured its gigantic vegetation. Again, the scene shifts, and all this northern hemisphere is a mass of ice, upon which one long snow-storm beats and drifts and falls, day and night, during a hundred years. The storm at last ceases; the snow melts; the icebergs and glaciers fall away: new heavens and a new earth arrive, fit for the home of man.* What mighty hand, what far-seeing mind, guided our earth, a drifting ship, without compass,

* A work lately published, called "The Pre-Glacial Man," considers the glacial epochs on the surface of the earth to result from the extreme elongation, at certain periods, of the transverse axis of the terrestrial orbit. The last period of this sort took place about 350,000 years ago, and continued about 270,000 years, ending 50,000 years ago. According to Denison's astronomy, when the excentricity of the earth's orbit was 10,500,000 miles, and winter in our hemisphere coincided with the earth's greatest distance from the sun, the mean cold of winter was 73° below its present temperature.

chart, or mariners, through these terrible dangers, and brought it to its present port in safety? Did the great God called Development do it; or shall we look higher?

Terrific forces, capable of blowing the earth to pieces, are now guided and restrained by the same great hand of power. Under our feet, a few miles down, there probably rolls an ocean of fire: above it, separated by a thin crust, rests the weight of five oceans. Let a crack occur, and an ocean pour down into this central furnace, and what could save us? Let the central fire lift the oceans a few thousand feet, and another universal deluge would come. Who sets a limit to the extremes of cold in winter, and heat in summer; so that the thermometer shall not fall to 100° below zero, or rise to 200° above it, but only oscillate between safe limits? We have a tornado occasionally, which blows down a few houses and trees. Let its force be but increased a little, and it would sweep away man and human civilization from the face of nature. Who says to the storm, to the sea, to the heat of summer, to the cold of winter, to plague, to famine, to fire, to pestilence, "Hitherto shalt thou come, but no further, and here shall thy power be stayed"?

I go out into the woods in the fair October days. Over a million flickering leaves, the innocent fires of autumn pour their flaming glories. Every imperial tint appears, — of scarlet and crimson, orange and yellow. The climbing vines hang from the branches their unbought draperies, more gorgeous than those of kings' palaces. The oak-leaves run up through their long gamut of browns. Little mosses cluster round the roots of the trees; a soft bed of tender green and gray lichens variegates their trunks. The clouds slide softly past the openings above; the brook circles and sweeps through light and darkness below. Who has bathed the world with this ineffable, indescribable beauty? If you come home after a few weeks' absence, and find your room arranged for you, — another picture on the walls, a new and pretty carpet under your feet, — you bless in your heart the thoughtful love which provided them. When we go out amid the infinite beauty of the advancing or declining year, and listen to the melodies of woods and winds and waters, — all new every hour, every moment, — shall we think they come by accident, or by some blind, cold law? I had rather be

"A pagan suckled in a creed outworn,"

amid "the intelligible forms of ancient poets," and "the fair humanities of old religion;" for the Greeks saw something divine in nature, — caught glimpses of naiads by the mountain streams, and of dryads hiding in the summer woods. Their ignorance was wiser than our cold reason, which disenchants nature of love and life. But wiser still the conception which finds God, the universal Father, above all, through all, and in all. Then earth becomes again alive; its soul is no more wanting. Again the little hills clap their hands; again the forests, lashing their branches in the storm, and the sea, rolling its long waves up the gleaming beach, call aloud upon God.

> " God! let the torrents, like a voice of nations,
> Answer; and let the ice-plains echo, God!
> God! sing, ye meadow streams, with gladsome voice;
> Ye pine groves, with your soft and soul-like sound;
> Ye signs and wonders of the elements
> Utter forth God, and fill the world with praise."

It is a law of nature, that, when we see adaptation, we infer design. When the geologist picks up a stone so smoothed and sharpened as to be adapted to do the work of a hatchet, he infers that it was probably designed for that object. But when he finds another and another, tens and hundreds, and with them other stones adapted for other human uses, his suspicion passes into certainty. But the world in which we live is crowded in every part with adaptations. Air, earth, sea, are adapted to furnish homes and food for various vegetables and animals. The lenses of the eye, and the optic nerve behind them, are adapted to the waves of light which roll from the sun, ninety millions of miles away. The eye is telescope and microscope, altering its own focus to suit the distance of the object. How admirably is the hand adapted to the work it has to do! It is a portable tool-chest, capable of the finest and the strongest work. The optical-instrument maker can find no better instrument than his thumb with which to grind the object-glass of a telescope. The blind man reads his letters with the ends of his fingers. Merely to enumerate the adaptations of the human body would require a work larger than that Chinese novel which, they say, occupied its author sixty years in writing, and was concluded in 162 folio volumes. The world is throughout woven into a great web of adaptations, dovetailed together, part fitting into part without friction, without jar. Did it come together thus without any foresight or design, — the growth of blind law? Then we may say that the roof which covers St. Peter's, with its trusses, its beams, its rafters, its braces, might have grown up by some law of development; for, for every mortise and every bearing in that roof, there are a million adaptations in the world around us. I hold in my hand, we will suppose, a volume. It is, let us say, Gibbon's "Decline and Fall of the Roman Empire." It narrates that vast transaction in a long, majestic succession of chapters, each teeming with knowledge and interest. I ask my atheist whence the book came. On his theory he might say: "It came by a chance process, without design. The lead out of which the types were made happened to get run into moulds, and by accident letters came at the end of each type. These types, whirled round in the vortex of circumstance, at last came together in a printing-office, and got themselves arranged by good luck in a printer's stick. Other materials, flowing together, developed themselves into paper and a printing-press; and by a natural law the letters were so arranged as to print this consecutive history. This," says my atheist, "is the philosophical explanation of the matter. No Faust invented printing; no great historian composed the story: it is unphilosophic to assume design, when development will explain it sufficiently." Is the atheist offended that I put such an absurd theory in his mouth? But what reason have we to attribute the mere record of Roman history to design, when you think no design apparent in Roman history itself, with all other human history; when you think that the wonderful story of earth and man drifted by a blind accident upon the stage of being? *

---

* Mr. Darwin's theory of the formation of species by natural selection is supposed, by some, to invalidate this whole argument for design. This theory is not yet science, but an hypothesis, which may or may not hereafter be accepted as science. But even though it should be proved altogether sound, it would not touch the theistic argument, which proceeds from adaptation to design. A few rudely formed stones, picked up in a formation containing no other vestige of man's presence, satisfy geologists of the past existence of mankind in the corresponding epoch, — so rooted in the human mind is the belief that adaptation proves design; for this is the only reason for believing it. The earth is a complete web of adaptations of part to part, constituting at last an order, a Kosmos, of beauty. Prove, if you can, that this has come by means of natural law: the question then returns, Who arranged and adapted those laws to produce this result? Did the laws of natural selection, and the struggle for existence, come by accident? Do we say, because a piece of cloth is

Such are the arguments by which the great thinkers of antiquity, — Socrates, Aristotle, and Plato, — and the great thinkers of modern times, — Descartes, Leibnitz, Newton, Malebranche, — have demonstrated the existence of the Deity. Because the idea of God is to be found in the human mind as an inherited possession; because, without this idea, the world is a chaos and the universe has no order; because the human mind, advancing inevitably from cause to cause, can only stop when it reaches the uncaused Source of all things; because the world itself, the more we study it, resolves itself more and more into a majestic order and a beauty inexplicable except on the assumption of a creative and loving Mind, the beginning and end of all things, — we find ourselves intellectually convinced of

---

made by a power-loom, that therefore it does not come by design? If we saw a watch so made that it would produce other watches, we should not think less skill shown in this construction, but more. Plutarch says (as quoted by Neander): "The ancients directed their attention simply to the divine in phenomena, and overlooked natural causes. The moderns turn away from that divine ground of things, and explain all things by natural causes. Both these views are partial, and the two ought to be combined." Because we can explain the machinery by which the hands of a clock turn, it does not follow that they are not designed to show the hour. If one accept the doctrine of the transmutation of species, without connecting it with final causes, we return to a world of chance, as absolutely empty of intelligence as that of Epicurus; and all that I have said above, in the illustration of Gibbon's History, is then fully justified.

the existence of a perfect Being, sole fair and sole true.

Yet, in reviewing these three main arguments for the existence of a supreme and perfect Being, we find that they all fail of producing full conviction, because they attempt to do by reasoning what reasoning is incompetent to perform; namely, to give us knowledge of that which we do not already know. The truth is, that we can only know God by revelation of himself to us, in us, around us. And these arguments have force only so far as they call attention to the fact that God comes and shows himself to us. We cannot, by searching, find him; but he finds us by revealing himself to us. The ontological argument, for example, is really this, — that there is deposited in the human mind, below all else, the conviction of the existence of a perfect Being, which is God revealing himself to us in the soul. The cosmological argument means, that God, in showing us finite and dependent existence, whispers to our thought that there is also necessary and independent being. And the power of the teleologic argument is, that it calls our attention to the vast web of nature; showing how part co-operates with part, and how a great universe of order and beauty arises out of this multitude of atoms, each by itself without power.

The doctrine of development, which has taken such an impulse in modern times, has not in itself the least atheistic tendency. Suppose the universe, at first, to have been a nebula, and all the present Kosmos to have come out of that nebula by the working of natural laws. All this must have happened in time, and had a beginning; for allowing millions and millions of years for each step, they, at last, carry us back to the formless nebula. Now, is not as much intelligence, as much power, as much love necessary to make a world-creating nebula, as to make a world? *

The argument resulting from all these arguments is therefore this. There arise in the human mind, by the necessity of its nature or condition, three ideas: 1. Of the Perfect. 2. Of the Necessary. 3. Of a Designing Cause. These three ideas cannot be separated. The Perfect Being, the Necessary Being, and the Designing Cause must be one. Consequently God reveals himself to us as the perfect, intelligent Cause of the universe. But this is a revelation, not a demonstration. Put into logical forms, as an argument, the power of it to convince is much less than when looked

---

* Professor Huxley, — in an article in "The Academy," Oct. 9th, 1869 — takes a similar view. He says, "The teleological and the mechanical views of nature are not, necessarily, mutually exclusive. On the contrary, the more purely a mechanist the speculator, is, the more firmly does he assume a primordial molecular arrangement, of which all the phenomena of the universe are consequences; and the more completely is he thereby at the mercy of the teleologist, who can always defy him to disprove that this arrangement was intended to evolve the phenomena of the universe."

at as a vision of the Almighty. For God does not wish to convince the unwilling of his existence, by a logical triumph over their reluctant understandings; but rather to show himself to the pure in heart, who desire to see him. He hides these truths from the wise and prudent, and reveals them unto babes.

We have thus glanced at the arguments by which the being of God is demonstrated. But now if you ask, "Why men believe in God?" I must give a different answer. Men believe in God, because they are made to believe in him, — because religion is natural to men, — because to trust in a Higher Power is a need of the human mind and heart. Men worship and adore God because their heart and their flesh cry out for him. Human nature has a craving for an infinite Upholder and Friend. Men do not eat and drink because books of physiology have taught them that food is necessary to support life, and have explained how it is transformed by the digestive organs into blood and flesh. They eat because they are hungry. So men do not worship because they have had the existence of God satisfactorily proved to their intellect; but because they are hungry for some spiritual and angelic food. No matter how low down men are, they feel this appetite; no matter how high they go, they do not outgrow it. They may sometimes fancy that there is something wise and manly in dispensing with religion. They may, in certain states of civilization and manners, stand apart from religious insti tutions. Some, like the great poet, Lucretius, may confound religion with superstition, and so reject both. But these are passing passions, eddies in the stream of thought: the great human current sweeps as steadily toward God, as the Amazon or Mississippi toward the ocean. While man's intellect, lost in the boundless varieties of things, seeks some unity, some central axis of belief, it can only rest in the idea of the Supreme Being. While man's will aspires upward, — ambitious of progress, growth, accomplishment, — it must always seek strength through faith in a Supreme Providence, guiding all souls in their appointed path. While man's heart yearns for a love, which no earthly affection can satisfy, it must turn to commune with the infinite Father. While human life is full of sorrow, men cannot dispense with that comfort which comes from the consolation of the Holy Spirit. As long as tyrants are to be resisted, slaves redeemed from their chains, the power of the wicked opposed, and the black depths of cruelty and selfishness uncovered to the day, — the lonely reformer, with no earthly helper, must trust in an infinite and almighty Justice. All goodness longs for God; all who love truth cry out for the perfect Truth; every thing noble within us ascends toward him. As we trust in the better and higher part of our nature, we believe more and more in God. So it is that faith is the evidence of things not seen, — so it is that the pure in heart at last see God.

Yes! it is no misuse of language to say that we can know God, as certainly as we know the outward world, or our own soul. It is by experience that all knowledge comes, not by reasoning. By repeated experience, through the senses, we know the world outside of us; by repeated experience, through the consciousness, we know the faculties and powers of our own soul; by repeated experience, through the reason, the conscience, and the spiritual nature, we come to know God. Those who only look down never see the sky. The inward eye, which sees God, is darkened by worldliness and sin. Until, we look up, in a disinterested love of truth and goodness, God remains only a problem and a possibility. The mere worship of form does not bring us near to him, but only that worship which is in spirit and in truth. But loyalty to conscience, trust in goodness, obedience to truth, — these unseal the eyes of the soul, and bring us into permanent communion with the Infinite and the Eternal.

We do not see God by merely opening our eyes: we must also open our heart. Prayer, devotion, the struggle for truth, the martyrdom to duty, — these bring us near to the Deity; these are the cherubic wings by which we ascend, passing the flaming bounds of space and time. To know God aright requires a great energy of soul, or a great humbleness of heart. Little children see God in their unsoiled simplicity and purity; their angels do always behold the face of our Father: and we must be converted from our worldliness, and become as little children, in order to perceive that infinite beauty. The greatest intellects have been most awed before the idea of God. "To know God aright," says Plato, "is difficult: to speak of him aright to others, almost impossible." "He veils himself behind his works," says Schiller, "and allows the atheist to deny his being by that very tolerance, showing his majestic presence more fully, than if he had struck him dead with a thunderbolt." "Who shall name him?" says Goethe.

> "Who shall name him?
> Who dare say
> 'I believe in him'?
> Who can deny him, —
> Who venture to affirm
> 'I believe in him not'?"

The grandest intellects have always bowed most profoundly before that Infinite Presence. But the child-like breast says, Abba! Father! This word "Abba," literally *Papa*, is in almost all languages the same, and the first word spoken by the infant; and so, in its highest signification, it is the first word spoken when we become once more little children, and enter the presence of the Heavenly Father. *

Let us hear the conclusion of the whole matter. The existence of God can never be proved satisfactorily to

---

* Paul did not translate the word, because he could not translate the infinitely tender associations which lay around it.

a doubting intellect; for the proof rests on spontaneous insights. But we come to know God by communion, just as we come to know the outward world. Only by acting on the outward world, and letting it react on us, do we become sure of its substantial reality. And so only by communion with God, speaking to him, receiving his answer, talking with him, beholding his face in righteousness, do we become at last as sure of the real presence of God as we are of the reality of the world.

CHAPTER III.

The Atheist's Theory of the Universe.

ATHEISM, pure and simple, which denies God, is a rare phenomenon, and always will be so. But atheism, in that form which omits God in its view of the world, is much more common. There are many theories of the universe which omit God. In speaking now of atheism, and its theory of the universe, I mean that atheism which omits and ignores in its manner of thought, a supreme and perfect Being, infinitely wise, holy, and good. It does not know any thing of a personal, self-conscious God, above all, through all, and in all things, — a God neither arbitrary, vindictive, cruel, nor indifferent to his creatures' welfare; but loving all, good and bad, saint and sinner, wise and foolish. The atheist must assume that the universe has always existed. For either it was created by some higher Being; or it made itself; or it has always existed. But the atheist denies that it was made by a higher Being; therefore the first alternative is out of the question. But it could not have made itself; because to make itself it must have existed: and, to be made by itself, it must have been non-existent. This theory, therefore, supposes that the world existed and did not exist, at the same moment, which is a contradiction. There remains, therefore, the third alternative, — that the world has existed always; and this all atheists (so far as I know) believe. But let us see what follows from that.

In speaking of the "atheist's theory of the universe," I wish to do the atheist perfect justice. I do not propose to use any hard names concerning him, or to try to make him odious or ridiculous, except so far as his own theory makes him so. I cannot undertake to defend him from any absurd consequences of his own argument; and if the logic of his position is weak, he must take the consequences.

The atheist, then, looks at the universe, and says, "There is no God." There is no supreme power; no universal presence; no infinite and perfect Being, intelligent, benevolent, conscious, and free. There are a great many finite beings, but no infinite Being. There is a vast swarm of imperfect creatures, but no perfection anywhere. The world was not created: it has always existed. God did not make it; and it could not have made itself out of nothing. Therefore, it has always been. This is fundamental in the theory of Atheism.

We perceive changes going on in the universe. We look at the earth, and find it is very different now from what it was a million, or a hundred million, years ago. There was a period when the continents were below the ocean; other periods in which they were covered with immense masses of ice; other periods, further back, in which the globe was a molten sea of fire, and a time, still more remote, when this mass of fiery liquid was probably flaming gas, a thousand times as vast. Now, if there is no God, what power has brought the earth through these changes?

The atheist replies, "Nature." But nature is a word; what does it mean? The atheist answers again, "The law of development. The earth has developed by natural laws from a fiery gas to a molten fluid; from a molten fluid to a body submerged by an ocean of water; from this to frozen continents; and at last, by various alternations, to what we now see, — animals, vegetables, and minerals; with climate, soil, air, water, food, suited to growth. Development did it all," says the atheist.

The Psalmist asks, "He who planted the ear, shall he not hear? He that formed the eye, shall he not see? He that teacheth man knowledge, shall he not know?" "By no means, "replies the atheist. "In this instance, the less has produced the greater; the cause here is lower than the effect. The power which made man a conscious and rational being, capable of knowledge, itself knows nothing, but acts unconsciously and blindly. The power which made man capable of generosity, affection, courage, ideality, faith, and hope, is itself incapable of even understanding these sentiments. The power which made man free, therefore capable of virtue, is itself bound fast by natural laws, and acts by a mechanical and chemical necessity, and so is incapable of virtue or goodness." In other instances, the greater makes the smaller; but never the smaller the greater. A man can make a machine to sing like a bird; but a bird cannot make a machine to speak like a man. Man can make a steam-hammer which can strike a blow of twenty tons' weight, and can also give a tap which will just crack a nut. But a steam-hammer cannot make a man. "As to the ear being made to hear, and the eye to see," says the atheist, "that is a mistake. Each is a happy accident, resulting from natural laws. Among a hundred million creatures, one happened to be born with an optic nerve, sensitive to light; and that gave him such an advantage in the struggle for life, that the eyeless animals disappeared, while he and his descendants remained. The ear is also a piece of good fortune. The ear has its drum, against which the waves of sound strike, making it vibrate. Behind the drum are little bones, the hammer-bone and the anvil-bone, and the stirrup-bone, through which the vibrations pass to a labyrinth which winds round and round in the bone, and is filled with a fluid in which the nerves of hearing terminate, each in its little sack. Every different sound, every articulate word, every varying note of the multitudinous sounds in the summer air, causes a different vibration in the fluid, and sends a different message to the brain; telling that it was the crow of a cock, the whistle of a robin, the cry of a boy, on the right or left, near or far, above or below. But this is all undesigned. If we see an ear-trumpet, we know it was designed to help the ear; but the ear itself was not designed for any thing. It came. If we see a pair of spectacles, we know they were designed to help the eyes: but the eyes were not designed for any thing; they came from the struggle for existence. When the Psalmist talked about God's planting the ear, and forming the eye, he had not read Darwin: if he had, he would have known that the ear and eye were not made with a purpose, but were developed accidentally."

Thus speaks our friend the atheist, uttering, as he imagines, the last word of science. But, even if we accept all of Mr. Darwin's theory, we do not in the least supply the place of a Creator. Grant that eye, ear, and hand, and all bodily organization, have been developed out of one original cell, — who made the cell, so that all these should be developed out of it? Who put into the primeval nebula its law of evolution, so that it should develop necessarily this Kosmos of wonder, beauty, and power? No theory which only shows how the world was made, can answer the question, Who made it? That remains to be solved the same as before.

Development does not mean a power or cause: it is only a process. We say that in a plant, the stalk is unfolded or developed out of the seed, the leaves out of the stalk, the flower out of the bud, the fruit out of the flower. This is development, — the way in which one part is unfolded out of another. But that is not a cause: it is only a method, a process. After we have said that the earth, as it now exists, was developed out of gas, we have not stated the cause of this phenomenon: we have only described the process. An immense, inscrutable Cause lies behind it. Some Power has done it all. What is that Power? To say nature or law or evolution, is merely describing how it happened, but does not bring you a single step nearer to the cause. When a man says that the earth has become what it is by development, he speaks as children do when they think they have explained the movements of an automaton, or the tricks of a juggler, by saying, "They are done by clock-work."

But let us grant (for the sake of argument), that there is in the universe some mysterious power or powers, hidden in matter, which have caused this development of fiery gas into an inhabited world. These powers must always have existed; for, if there was a time when there was no such power in matter, as there was no power to create it, it must have created itself, which is impossible. But it has not always existed, for development, going on for ever, would have at last produced an infinitely perfect Being, that is a God, which is contrary to the atheist's hypothesis. The atheist is therefore held by this dilemma. He must either deny that this active principle of development inheres in the material universe; or he must admit that it has existed for ever in it: and, if active for ever, it must, in infinite time, have developed an infinitely perfect Being. And so he must either give up his theory of development, or admit the existence of God.

No one will deny that intelligence is superior to unintelligence. A conscious intelligent force, freely choosing to create, is higher in the scale of existence than a blind force, necessarily creating, with no plan, and for no end. It would seem, therefore, that if the laws of nature are laws of development, ever tending upward, unfolding higher forms out of lower ones, they would, in an infinite period, unfold a perfect Being, — intelligent, conscious, and free. Those who do not accept, with the theists, a personal conscious God as the cause of creation, are bound to accept him as the result of development. If God is not at the beginning, he must arrive at the end. The theory of Darwin is a perpetual progress. The law of natural selection always chooses the better, and refuses the worse. Its maxim is, "To him that hath shall be given." But why should it stop with man? Why terminate its career just at this point? Given an infinite period for its work, and why not produce a perfect Being; that is, God?

Mathematicians, however, have calculated, from laws governing the process of radiated heat, that the earth can only have occupied a definite period in cooling down from a gas to its present state.* The atheist may therefore say that time enough has not yet elapsed to develop a perfect Being on the surface of the earth. A God, however, it may be hoped, will arrive at last, on this theory. No limit can be set to this principle of evolution, which has already given us the mineral, vegetable, and animal kingdoms; and in the last has gone up through radiata, mollusca, articulata, to fishes reptiles, birds, and mammalia, and so arrived at man. During this finite period, it has produced the human mind on this planet. But if, during a finite period, matter has developed finite mind on this particular planet, then, throughout the infinite universe, during an infinite period, it ought to have developed infinite mind. Therefore, if God did not create the universe, the universe must have created God. In either case God exists, and atheism is refuted.

The only escape from this reasoning which I can discover, is the assumption that all things revolve in a great circle. The atheist may say that just as the seed is unfolded into a plant, and then produces flower and

---

* Professor Sir William Thomson has calculated the probable age of the crust of the earth to be about 98,000,000 of years; which must, therefore, comprehend the whole geological history of our planet. — *Philosophical Magazine*, 1863.

From Professor Houghton's fourth lecture on geology, we learn that it took the earth 350,000,000 years to cool from 2,000° to 200° centigrade; and that to cool from 212° Fahrenheit to 77°, required 2,298,000,000 of years. — *Pre-Glacial Man.*

fruit, which at last die, leaving only seed, to begin again the same career, — so it is with the universe. A nebula turns to a world; the world produces human beings with minds, hearts, and souls, — with an infinite hope and inexhaustible capacities, — these die, and the world goes to gas and nebula again, and again passes from nebula to another world.

It may be so: it is a supposable case that we journey through this dreary, empty, blind round, — coming from nowhere, and going nowhere. This, I think, must be the atheist's theory of the universe. Either the universe has always been growing better, and then, in an infinite series of years, it would have developed perfection, — that is, God, — which the atheist denies; or, secondly, it must have been always growing worse, and then, in an infinite series of years, it would have annihilated itself, which it has not done; or else, thirdly, it has been going round and round, from better to worse, and from worse to better again, for ever.

If this is the atheist's theory, he looks out into an awful universe. It is black with a terrible fate, which grinds blindly on and on, crushing human hope under its merciless wheels. That is the peculiarity of atheism, — that it is without hope. The Scripture, with its wonderful power of condensing into a single sentence whole volumes of philosophy and theology, says (Eph. ii. 10), "without hope in the world, and atheists." That is the dreadful doom of the atheist, — to lose hope. He does not lose pleasure: he retains the power of enjoying the present moment. He does not lose conscience: he may be a very conscientious man, doing what he thinks is right, and having that kind of satisfaction which always comes with right doing. He may be a very benevolent man; kind-hearted to the sufferer, affectionate in his family, a good neighbor. But he is a hopeless man.

No doubt there is an instinctive hope natural to men, of which some have more and others less. This is a part of their organization. But hope, as a conviction, as a habit of thought, comes only from faith in God, — faith in a perfect Being. It is God, who carries to perfection all that we see of good in man; the Supreme Being, head of the universe, perfect in power, in wisdom, and in goodness. He is a Being who loves every one of his creatures with a perfect love; a Providence guiding the world, and leading it forward from bad to good, from good to better. Only this faith in God creates hope in man and in the world, as a living principle, as a permanent conviction. Believing thus in God, we believe in progress; believe that all things are growing better. We believe that all that is dark will become clear, all that seems evil now will become good hereafter; that life is good, and death is good; that nature and man are both good; that evil is a disease which must pass away. We believe that sin is to be cured, and the sinner saved, and that heaven here is to pass up into heaven hereafter. This is the great, luminous, far-reaching hope which arises out of faith in God, and which nothing else can give. Science cannot give it; because science only observes and classifies present phenomena. Philosophy, separated from spiritual insight, and judging only by sense, cannot give it; for philosophy can only see things as they are, not as they are to be. But faith in God puts a principle of progress into science and philosophy, — feeds them both at their roots with a generous expectation. For neither science, art, philosophy, nor civilization can move forward or make progress without hope. Therefore, where atheism or irreligion prevails, civilization stops, human progress is arrested, science becomes languid, art dies.

When Christ came, hope lay dead in the hearts of men. The world seemed to have come to an end. Life was empty. All faith in the old gods had died, and the Augurs and Chief Pontiffs argued against the truth of their own religion.* The purest and best of men were the most unhappy. Aurelius Antoninus, one of the noblest and most virtuous of mankind, was, says Niebuhr, one of the gloomiest. It seemed no

---

* Cicero, in his dialogue "De Naturâ Deorum," makes Cotta, the Pontifex Maximus, while accepting the State religion in his quality of its Chief Priest, argue as a philosopher against the reality of divination by the entrails of beasts, the voice of crows, and the casting of lots. While professing to believe in the gods as a good citizen, he denies the validity of every argument for their existence, and ascribes the world to nature as its cause.

longer worth while to live. Amid this utter hopelessness came the Christian faith, and its life was the light of men. Listen to Paul, — a poor Jew, hated by his own people, despised by the Gentiles, the object of derision, persecution, abuse, wherever he went; but full of the loftiest hope, and saying in tones which still ring through the centuries like the blast of a trumpet, "What shall separate us from the love of God? Tribulation, or distress, or persecution, or famine, or nakedness, or peril, or sword? In all these things we are more than conquerors, through him that loved us. For I am persuaded that neither death, nor life, nor angels, nor principalities, nor powers; nor things present, nor things to come; nor height nor depth, nor any other creature, shall be able to separate us from the love of God, which is in Christ Jesus our Lord."

The atheist has no hope. He looks at the heavens. He sees a majestic order, — planets revolving round suns, stars around other stars, all moving with perfect regularity along their prodigious pathways. But he sees no mind creating and controlling this vast order. He sees rules, but no Ruler; law, but no Lawgiver. Star-eyed science brings us from its vast excursions only the tidings of despair. The universe is a vacuum, empty of God; rolling on for ever and ever, without reason, without meaning, without purpose, without end. The heavens do not declare to him the glory of God, but only the glory of Sir Isaac Newton or La Place. This is as if one should open Homer or Shakespeare, not to be moved by the genius of the author, but to wonder at the intelligence of the pupils who have learned to spell "but" and "and" out of the volume.

The atheist looks at the earth. Everywhere he sees adaptation; but he sees no design. Force and Matter, two blind Cyclops, have gone to work in a fit of intoxication, and tossing things madly to and fro, instead of destroying every thing, have created, in their ignorant struggle, this beautiful world. What Force and Matter have made, they will one day destroy again.

The atheist goes with a great poet to visit the vale of Chamouni. They stand together on the Flegère, looking across the valley to watch the coming day. They see the morning-star pausing over the "bald, awful, sovereign front" of the mountain. They see the mountain rising, dark and dread, silently out of its silent sea of pines. They watch the rosy dawn creeping over the untouched snow of its summit. They observe the granite obelisks around, piercing the dark sky like wedges. They look at the light, as it creeps down the vast fields of snow, crosses the deep ravines, and lights up the five glaciers, "for ever shattered and the same for ever." The poet, inspired by the sublime scene, sings his hymn of praise to the Maker of the mountain, and that hymn becomes immortal. The atheist, who is a man of taste, admires the poem, and sees in it the work of a creative mind. That could not have come by chance. But Coleridge himself, and the sublime scene which inspired him, these required no creative mind to produce them. They were the result of accident, or "natural selection."

The atheist sits before the Dresden Madonna. He drinks in the tender beauties of the mother, — the wonderful expression, depth below depth, in the eyes of the child. Day after day he visits it, and finds its mysterious charm ever more inexplicable and inexhaustible. In the genius of its author, he sees evidence of almost prophetic wisdom, and a boundless power of imagination. The work of Raphael, he knows, could only come from a creative mind; but Raphael himself, he thinks, came from no mind at all, — only from force and matter, working by natural selection. He knows that force and natural selection could never have made the picture; but he thinks that they made the painter of the picture. Blind laws could not even have made the brush, or ground the colors, or stretched the canvas, — far less have created, touch after touch, that divine beauty; but the soul which did all this and more, — that was the work of accident, force, or, if you prefer the phrase, development. This is the theory of the atheist.

Alexander VI. sits at Rome, a monster of licentiousness, avarice, falsehood, and cruelty. He poisons his own cardinals, that he may seize their estates. He excels his predecessors, Nero and Tiberius, in every mad excess of wickedness, with which they had polluted the palace and throne. Meantime, by his orders, Savonarola, at Florence, — noble reformer, holy prophet, purest of men, — is confined in prison, to be executed in the morning. The saint kneels on the cold stone, and prays to God to support him; and God sends hope and peace into his heart. But the atheist looks into the cell, and says, "Fool! there is no God. Matter and Force made the world; Matter and Force rule it. There is no help in God. The only help is in praying to the man — half beast, half devil — who sits at Rome. Fall down and worship him, and save your life; for if you die, that is the end of you. Pray to Borgia; he can hear you: but do not pray to God; for there is no God on earth or in heaven to listen to the prayers of the just."

Uncle Tom, on the plantation of Legree, finds himself in a hell of torture. Torn from his home, sold to a brute more cruel than the tigers (for they only kill for food, and do not torture for pleasure), worn by toil in the day, starved and frozen at night, — his only comfort is that God, the righteous Judge, sees all and rules all. He cries to him, lays all his grief before that infinite pity, and finds peace in the all-embracing Father's love. But the atheist comes and says: "Nonsense! you are talking to a deaf and cold universe, in which there is no God. I have looked for him through my eight-foot telescope, and did not find him among the stars. I have looked for him with my powerful Spencer's microscope, and do not find him in the elemental matter. Even the spectral analysis does not reveal him. He cannot help you. He has no ear to pity, and no arm to save. Flatter Legree, and aid him in torturing other victims: that is your only course. He can hear you; but God hears no one."

Two young men go to the war, to fight for the Union against the Rebellion. One goes from his happy home, his delightful studies, his present full of joy, his future full of promise; because the voice of Duty calls him away. His dying father puts his hand on his head, and says, "Go, my son; do your duty; leave me here to die." His mother, who cannot let the summer breeze visit him too rudely, says, "Go, my boy, to the hardship of the camp, the foot-sore, dusty march, the sickness, the loneliness, the prison at Andersonville, the torturing death on the field of battle. Go; for it is your duty." And so he goes, with no light heart, but with a serious purpose, and lies buried beneath an upturned sod in the Virginia woods. The other goes too; but as a politician, to get influence and office by and by; or he goes as a speculation, — to make money. He gets the easiest position, and seldom joins his regiment. He cheats the soldiers of their pay, and their rations, and fills his pockets with plunder. On the day of battle, he has business at the rear, and keeps himself safe. He comes home, gets himself made a Brigadier, and runs for Congress. The atheist says, "He is the wiser of the two; for he, at any rate, has got something, and is alive, but the other has become carbon and hydrogen, and is gone för ever."

The husband lays in the earth the dear remains of his best-beloved one. They have lived together a few happy days: his heart has grown purer each hour in her sweet society. All his earthly hope was in the joy of her smile. And now she lies before him, pale and cold, Decay's effacing fingers not yet having swept away the lingering lines of beauty from her lip and brow. In this hour of mortal anguish, his heart and his flesh cry out for the living God. And God, hearing his prayer, puts an immortal hope into his heart. The heavens are opened, and he sees his darling alive, and more alive than ever, in that infinite home. He feels her presence near: he is overshadowed by her immortal love; and his agony changes to peace. Then comes the atheist, and says, "What a fool to think she is alive! She was a compound of hydrogen and carbon brought together, and organized by Matter and Force, and created by a process of evolution. Now she is carbon and hydrogen again in an unorganized state. She has gone for ever. Eat and drink; for tomorrow you will die too. Do not pray to God: he is nothing but the Kosmos itself. This is the religion of all men of science."

The atheist looks at the fact of evil in the world, and so denies the existence of a perfect God. "If a perfect God has made the world, how can the world be imperfect?" he says: "how can perfection produce imperfection?" and he chuckles over his triumphant logic. According to our ideas, no doubt the world is very imperfect. So the fly, beating his head against a glass window, might say, "What an imperfect work of art is this house! It ought to have had open windows for me to fly out of!" So the new-fledged bird, picking at an unripe berry, might say, "What an imperfect world, in which the berries are made bitter!" The countryman, going into the Gobelin factory, and seeing the workmen spending years of labor on what seems only a coarse and ragged figure in the tapestry, may say, "What imperfect and inferior work is this?" But wait, little fly, till you can understand for what the house was made; wait, little bird, till you can see your berry ripen in the advancing summer; wait, critic, till you behold the other side of the tapestry; and wait, atheist, until you can comprehend the plans of an infinite God. Thus much we can see, — that evil is continually used, as a dark material, out of which good is manufactured; that the mysteries of life prove the greatness of the soul, by showing that it can reach out to laws and facts, which it cannot yet comprehend. To the theist, these mysteries, planted in the mind, are a promise of immortality. For if God has put into our very reason difficulties which are insoluble here, is not this a promise that they shall be solved hereafter? The human mind is so made, that it must ask questions, to which it cannot find an answer in this life: is there not then another, where these problems will find their solution?

The atheist may say, "Suppose all you say is correct, what then? My theory of the universe may be discouraging; it may take away all hope, all consolation in trouble, all support in bereavement: but what then? Is it, or is it not true? that is the question." I admit that this is the question. But I consider it a strong argument against any theory, that it leads to despair. The best proof of a theory is, that it harmonizes all facts, reconciles difficulties, and explains the universe so as to leave the mind at peace. The theory which satisfies the mind is most probably the true one; that which leaves it dissatisfied is probably the false one. Now, the belief in the perfect God leaves both the mind and heart at peace. It produces activity of head and hand, joy in existence here, hope as regards hereafter. It gives unity to the world, by filling it with God. It gives a purpose to life, as leading us up to him. The believer in God is happy, hopeful, and strong. The tender and timid woman, inspired by this faith, goes willingly to die. But who ever died a martyr in the cause of atheism? Perhaps some may have done so for the love of truth; and an honest belief may lead even an atheist to die for his convictions. But what a terrible martyrdom, — to die in the cause of Despair; to die as an apostle of Annihilation; to die, in order to persuade men that there is no infinite wisdom to guide us, no infinite power to protect us, no infinite Father to love us, no perfect beauty and goodness for us to love! Once in a while, an exceptional man, from simple conscience, may dare to die for this dreary creed. But the noble army of martyrs always goes to death in the cause of faith, not of doubt; of a glad hope and trust in that which is perfect and divine. And the fact that a theory satisfies the soul is a proof of its truth; for mental satisfaction is the natural result of seeing the truth. The best proof that any theory of physiology is true, is that, when put in practice, it leaves the body in health; without sickness or pain, contented and satisfied. The best proof that any intellectual theory is true, is that, in the long run, it leaves the mind contented and satisfied, and the heart at rest.

The atheist's theory of the universe leaves the soul empty and the heart dead. It explains nothing: it leaves us without hope. But faith in an infinite and perfect God tends to elevate and vitalize the soul, — to make man stronger, purer, and wiser. It leads us from the finite to the infinite. And so we end, with the poet in saying: —

"All are but parts of one stupendous whole,
Whose body nature is, and God the soul.
That, changed through all, and yet in all the same,
Great in the earth as in the starry frame,
Warms in the sun, refreshes in the breeze,
Glows in the stars, and blossoms in the trees,
Lives through all life, extends through all extent,
Spreads undivided, operates unspent.
To him, no high, no low, no great, no small;
He fills, he bounds, connects, and equals all.

Safe in the hand of one disposing Power,
Or in the natal or the mortal hour,
All nature is but art unknown to thee;
All chance, direction which thou canst not see;
All discord, harmony not understood:
All partial evil, universal good."*

---

* It has been objected to some of the illustrations in this discourse, that they unfairly represent the atheist as incapable of generous and disinterested actions. I have conceded, very willingly, that men may be found professing atheism whose lives are magnanimous, conscientious, and good. But it is not the tendency of doubt or denial of spiritual things to elevate the soul or nerve it to great achievements. A few knights-errant of atheism may do deeds of chivalric heroism; but the noble army of martyrs never graduates from that school.

CHAPTER IV.

IMPERFECT AND PERFECT THEISM.

THE subject of the present chapter is, Imperfect and Perfect Theism.

Perfect theism is the belief in a perfect Being, above all things, through all things, and in all things. A perfect Being is one who unites in himself all the good which belongs to finite beings, and carries that good to perfection. Existence is a good belonging to finite beings, without which no other good is possible. But the existence of finite beings is contingent and dependent. Existence, made perfect, becomes necessary and independent. God's being is therefore necessary being, or, as we now say, He is the absolute Being. Again, reason or intelligence is a good belonging to finite beings. Carried to perfection, it becomes infinite wisdom or omniscience. Again, power is a good; and this, carried to perfection, is omnipotence. Once more, the finite being becomes more perfect, as, by means of a higher organization and finer senses, it comes more fully into communion with nature. A perfect communion with nature would be what we call omnipresence, or God all in all. In the same way, a perfect Being must be perfect in love, or an infinite Giver; perfectly free, or not limited by an external or internal force stronger than himself; and therefore perfectly self-conscious, or entirely disengaged from blind impulses and instincts.

If this is perfect theism, it is easy to point out the different varieties of imperfect theism. We shall proceed to do this. Any view of God which limits his power, wisdom, goodness, freedom; or makes these doubtful,—is, so far, an imperfect form of theism.

Of these varieties of imperfect theism, we will specify the following:—

I. Nature-worship.—Theism appears in this form in many of the Hymns of the Vedas, and in the Gathas of the Zend-Avesta. God is contemplated as immersed in nature,—personified, but not personal,—as a presence in the sun, the winds, the fire, the water, the clouds, the dawn, the stars. He is thus a blind, though often a beneficent, force. He is *in* nature, and so far is truly conceived. But he is not *above* nature; and therefore is neither intelligent, personal, nor free.

II. Polytheism.—This is the first reaction against naturalistic pantheism, and the first development of personality. Will, choice, intelligence, benevolence,—all may appear in this conception of Deity. But unity, infinity, and universality are absent. The polytheistic view conceives of God correctly, as *through* all things; but not as *above* all things. A group of finite deities, all imperfect, do not make an infinite Deity. In the Greek mythology, — the highest form of polytheism, — the gods are only larger, more beautiful, more intelligent, and more powerful men and women. But all are limited by defects, weaknesses, and imperfections.

III. IDOLATRY. — Polytheism almost always ultimates in idolatry. But idolatry, in its essence, often appears in Christianity as well as in paganism.

In giving a bodily form to God, and locating him in one place, idolatry limits his omnipresence. Then God acts through the visible idol, where that is, and does not act elsewhere. And so when we speak of the sabbath as a holy day, of the church as a holy place, of the Bible as a holy book, we are in danger of idolatry; just as Catholics are when they worship the Virgin of Fourvières at Lyons, San Gennaro at Naples, or St. Lawrence at Genoa. Reverence for what is good, true, and noble is not idolatry. To reverence the truth in the Bible, or to love the rest, peace, and worship of the Lord's day, — is not idolatry. To reverence St. Francis of Assisi, or any other good man, is not idolatry. But we begin to idolize men, books, creeds, churches, whenever we worship the body and the outward form, instead of the spirit which it contains and conveys. Therefore Jesus teaches his disciples to begin their prayer by saying, "Our Father, who art in heaven;" therefore he tells the woman of Samaria, "Neither in this mountain, nor yet in Jerusalem, shall men worship the father." Idolatry is worshipping the form instead of the spirit, the means instead of the end, the body instead of the soul.

IV. Pantheism. — The opposite error to that of idolatry is pantheism, and this is also an imperfect theism. Idolatry confines God to places, times, and forms: pantheism puts him in all things, which is right; but goes further, and says that all things are God, which is wrong. When we make all things equally divine, we take away all moral character from the Deity, and he becomes only the blind soul of nature. Then we destroy also morality in man. Right and wrong become equally a part of God; and sin is a divine manifestation, no less than goodness.

No doubt, true theism comes very close to pantheism. It grazes pantheism, but avoids it. Many texts in the New Testament have an extremely pantheistic sound; but none express the fundamental idea of pantheism. When Paul says of God, "From whom, and through whom, and to whom are all things;" when he teaches that God is "above all, and through all, and in us all;" when he tells the Athenians that "in him we live and move and have our being," — he teaches the truth in pantheism which corrects the mechanical theory of the universe. God is not like a mechanic, who makes the world out of some foreign substance, and then sets it in motion, and goes away and leaves it. He is the present, continued, constant Creator. The mechanical view implied in the account of creation of Genesis is corrected by Jesus. The book of Genesis says that God "rested on the seventh day." Jesus says (John v. 17), "My Father worketh hitherto" (ἕως ἄρτι, *down to this time*). God is the immanent, and not the transient, cause of the universe. He creates it, not as one candle is lighted from another, but as the image of the sun is made on the surface of water. The candle lights the other, and then is taken away. The sun continues to create its image, without cessation. Hildebert, in his hymn, says of the Deity: —

"Super cuncta, subter cuncta:
Extra cuncta, intra cuncta;
Intra cuncta, nec inclusus;
Extra cuncta, nec exclusus;
Super totus præsidendo,
Subter totus sustinendo;
Extra totus complectendo,
Intra totus in complendo," &c.

This is the true view of God in all things, and all things in God. But when it is carried a single step further, and we say that God is every thing, and that every thing is God, we confound all distinctions. Then right and wrong, good and evil, light and darkness, man and God, are fatally confused. Then a moral and spiritual death comes over the soul and over society, as the history of Hindoo theism has shown.

V. Nescience. — The next form of imperfect theism is found in the metaphysical doctrine of nescience. This doctrine admits the existence of God, but denies that we can know any thing about him. This is the doctrine of such writers as Hamilton, Mansel, and Herbert Spencer; the latter, a thinker much admired, but who, though an acute metaphysician, seems to us to be a poor philosopher. He considers an "unknown God" as the highest attainment of theology and philosophy. He says: "The deepest, widest, and most certain of all facts is that the power which the universe manifests is wholly inscrutable." It will be seen that this is using against theology its own favorite doctrine of mystery. Theologians, when pressed with the absurdities of their systems, and shown that their creeds contradict the simplest laws of reason, nature, common sense, and every instinct of the soul, have cried out, "It is a mystery! We must believe it; but we cannot understand it." And now Mr. Spencer and others say, "Yes: all theology is a mystery. We can know nothing about it. We must let it all alone, and devote ourselves to practical matters, to things of this world. God exists; but we know nothing about him. Therefore we have nothing to do with theology or religion, and cannot believe any thing about either." Thus mystery, pushed too far, has destroyed belief.

The origin of this doctrine of nescience seems to be a confusion between understanding a fact and comprehending it. We know a great many things which we cannot comprehend. We know that space is infinite; but who can comprehend infinity? The ideas of infinite space and infinite time are perfectly simple and intelligible notions. We understand perfectly both ideas, but we comprehend neither. Our mind, being finite, can by no possibility comprehend the infinite. That is, our knowledge of it is correct in quality, but limited in quantity. We hold it firmly, but cannot grasp it all. A child knows his father correctly; but how imperfectly does he comprehend him! So I can know God truly; I can understand truly what infinite wisdom, power, and goodness mean; but how little do I comprehend of their vast range, of their immense plan, of their enormous depth, breadth, height! "Who by searching can find out God? who can find out the Almighty *to perfection?*"

VI. LAW AND CAUSE. — The next imperfect theism makes of the Deity a law, and not an intelligent Cause. Natural science looks only at facts and laws, and sometimes forgets that a law is only a method of working, and that behind all law there must be power. A legislature passes a law declaring that no intoxicating liquor shall be sold in any of the shops of the State; and presently no liquor is sold in some places, while it continues to be sold in other places. Behind the law, in one place, is a power — namely, the power of public opinion — which enforces the law. Behind the law in another place is no such power, and therefore it is not enforced.

Natural science observes facts, and infers laws. It

observes, for example, that the best organized plants and animals live, while others die; that these best organized plants, by an organic law, communicate their qualities to their successors, and so form a permanent variety. Hence it infers the law of progress, by which the strongest creatures live and the weaker die. Thus, all the varieties of plants and animals, and all the progress of these from the lowest germ and cell up to man, are accounted for by law. Be it so. Theology has no quarrel at all with science, while science shows how things come to exist. But to show how they come, is not to show why they come. Law is not power; law is not intelligence; law is not goodness. Law itself implies a law-maker and a law-enforcer; and, if the law works for the general good, that the law-maker and law-enforcer is also beneficent. That is, the law implies wisdom, power, and goodness behind it.

Science, therefore, produces imperfect theism, not while it is genuine science, but when it goes out of its province of observing facts and inferring laws, and assumes that these facts and laws are sufficient to account for the universe.

VII. Positivism. — Another imperfect theism is positivism. Positivism declares that we only know what we get at through the senses; and as the senses only perceive phenomena, that we can only know phenomena. It declares that there is nothing but phenomena and their succession, of which we can know any thing. Of causes we can know nothing, but only of phenomena and their laws.

The fatal weakness of this system, wherever it comes to light, — whether as taught by Comte in its integrity, or taught in a more diluted form by others, — is that it assumes that there is only one way by which knowledge can enter the mind; namely, by the senses. It assumes it, but does not prove it, or seriously try to prove it.

The Bible says, and says correctly, that "spiritual things are spiritually discerned." Man has various organs by which he discerns various realities. Each class of realities is discerned through its own organ. In externals, we know this well enough. We never expect to see with our hands, or to smell with our ears. We know that we cannot do a sum in the rule of three by our nose, or taste with our tongue the proper translation of a Greek sentence. Visible things, we know, are optically discerned, by the eyes; audible things are discerned audibly, by the ears; tangible things are discerned by the touch; logical things are detected by the reason; emotions of the soul are perceived by the consciousness; historical facts are reported by the memory. We do not deny the existence of Julius Cæsar, because we cannot touch him; nor the fragrance of a rose, because we cannot hear it. Nor do we deny the existence of hope and fear, love and hatred, because these cannot be perceived by the senses. Why, then, doubt the reality of spiritual things, because they must be spiritually discerned?

VIII. Theology of Will. — But there is yet another form of imperfect theism, which is more common. It is that popular theology which makes God a tyrant, and man a slave; which divorces the divine will from his justice and his love, and so makes it an arbitrary and despotic will. The powerful Augustinian theology, revived and renewed by Calvin, taught that God from the beginning created some men to be saved and some to be lost. Without any regard to their goodness or their wickedness, he saves some, because he chooses to do so; without any regard to their wickedness or their goodness, he damns others, because he chooses to do so. This substitutes, in the place of the infinite and perfect God, an arbitrary, imperfect, and wilful Power. Infinite will — divorced in our thought from infinite justice, wisdom, and love — is less perfect than infinite will allied to these. The God of Calvin is therefore an imperfect God, unable or unwilling to save all his creatures; able and willing to save only a part of them.

Calvinism, in its form of election and arbitrary decrees, is fast passing away. It does not exist in the Episcopal or Methodist Churches, hardly among the Orthodox Congregationalists and New-School Presbyterians; and holds its place with difficulty among the Old-School Presbyterians in the South and South-west. But one doctrine which deforms theology and dishonors God, still remains in all the orthodox churches. It is the doctrine of everlasting punishment, in the other world, for the sins committed in this life. No church, claiming to be orthodox, has yet dared to repudiate this awful doctrine, which is more injurious to the character of the Almighty than all the blasphemies of the impious, and all the denials of the atheist. For what does it assert? That God keeps his children in existence for ever, merely to torment them for ever; inflicting on each one an amount of suffering infinitely greater than all the pangs of the martyrs, and all the agonies of the sufferers, who have been in the world since the world began. Add together the tortures inflicted by the tyrants and despots in all time, the *auto-da-fes* of the Inquisitions, the cruel torments of every battle-field of history, the solitary sufferings from disease, accident, moral and mental anguish, — add them together, and when an equivalent to all has been suffered by one soul, his suffering has only begun. All the sufferings of time added together, are finite; and if they end at last in universal and infinite bliss, — no matter how far off that consummation may be, — they are mathematically and logically nothing when compared with the succeeding joy. But let one soul suffer to all eternity, and his solitary suffering infinitely outweighs the anguish borne in all time in all the worlds of the universe. If suffering is finite, and final bliss is universal and infinite, then suffering disappears, and is reduced to nothing. But if suffering is infinite, then evil shares the throne of the universe with God, then God is no longer universal sovereign. "He wills to have all men saved," says the Scripture. Is he unable to save them? Either he is deficient in goodness, and so does not wish to save them; or he is deficient in wisdom, and does not know how to save them; or he is deficient in power, and is not able to save them. In either case, he is not a perfect Being. Thus the doctrine of everlasting punishment dethrones God, and leaves him the servant of some dark fate outside of himself.

It is no answer to this, to say that God allows evil to exist here in time. For we have seen that all the sufferings of time are mathematically nothing, compared with the bliss of eternity. All finite suffering, however great, is as nothing when compared with everlasting happiness afterward.

We will close this chapter by giving a brief *résumé* of our argument thus far.

If we are asked, "Why do you believe in God?" we may give the following answer: —

I believe in God, because I am made to believe in him. If I became an atheist, I should be obliged to silence the voice of my soul, the instincts of my higher being, the voice of my reason, the dictates of nature, the aspirations of the spirit rising above the finite to the infinite, the longings of my heart for an almighty and perfect Friend. I am so made that I have no peace, no rest, no satisfaction in the present, no hope in the future, but in the faith that — above all that is dark, blind, and mechanical in the universe; behind all that is mysterious and sad, — there sits supreme one infinite Master, who is at the same time an infinite Benefactor, an endless Lover of his creatures.

Secondly, I believe in God because I see everywhere, in nature and the outward world, the proofs of a boundless intelligence. I see everywhere adaptation, and infer design; everywhere order, law, beauty, harmony. All Nature sings a song of praise to God. Opening spring, which unbinds the sod, announces his coming, with numerous flowers, birds, and returning life. The long summer days, filled with joy, speak of him. Him the abounding autumn, him the solemn winter, proclaim. His praise is sung by the winds, which blow from four quarters of the heavens; and by the majesty and terror of the storm. The mighty ocean chants his praise in its tumultuous surges, and its immeasurable smile. The mountains, great sentinels of nature, in their perpetual calm and snowy purity, praise God with their sky-piercing peaks. Coming day, and the rising sun, pouring light over the earth, tell of his goodness; and night, with its solemn multitude of fires, shows to us his infinite power. I believe in God, because nature is full of him; in all its order, its beauty, its manifold variety, its infinite adaptation.

Again, I believe in God because the universal testimony of man, from the dawn of time, bears witness to the divine reality. Faintly or clearly, all people, nations, and languages have seen the presence of God in the world, — sometimes, as in a glass darkly, involved in superstition and error; sometimes in clearer light and beauty. Polytheism and monotheism, Jew and Gentile, Brahmin and Buddhist; the negro of Africa with his Fetich; the Scandinavian with his faith in Valhalla; the solemn mystery of the Egyptian shrines with their long arcades of sphinxes and obelisks; the Acropolis at Athens glittering in its snowy marble beauty, its exquisite temples, its innumerable statues; Rome with its altars; the isles of the ocean; the ancient worship of Mexico and Peru, and the Great Spirit of the Indian, — all attest the fact, that wherever man has lived, he has looked out of time into eternity, and has seen some gleams of a divine power above and beyond the earth.

Once more, I believe in God, because the wisest and best of the race have risen always out of superstition on the one side, and unbelief on the other, to the sight of one infinite and perfect Being. The Hymns of the Vedas, in their highest strains, announce one supreme God. The great teacher of ancient Persia, Zoroaster, discloses the God of light and truth and goodness, as the highest power. Greece, by the voice of her best and greatest philosophers, announces the same truth. No one in the Old World taught a purer theism than Socrates; no one demonstrated the purity and perfection of the Deity more plainly than Aristotle. Plato says, "Around the King of all, are all things; and he is the cause of all good." Euripides declares, "God sees all things, and is himself unseen." The Pythagoreans said, "God is one. He is not, as some suppose, outside this frame of things, but within it. In all the entireness of his being, he is in the whole circle of existence, surveying all nature, and blending in harmonious union the whole; Giver of light in heaven, and Father of all; the mind and life of the whole world; Mover of all things." Sophocles says: —

"One in truth, one is God,
Who made both heaven and the far-reaching earth,
And ocean's blue wave and the mighty winds.
But many of us mortals, deceived in heart,
Have set up for ourselves, as a consolation in our affliction,
Images of the gods, of stone or wood or brass or gold or ivory,
And worship these with vain sacrifices."

And Orpheus, as quoted by Clement of Alexandria, says: "I shall utter to whom it is lawful; but let the doors be closed against all the profane. Walk in the straight path to the immortal and only King of the universe. For he is one, self-proceeding. From him all things come: his power is in all. No mortal sees him; but he sees all."

And so Cicero says of the Romans: "Some nations, conscript fathers, excel us, — as do the Spaniards in numbers, the Gauls in physical strength, the Carthaginians in cunning, the Greeks in art; but we, the

Romans, surpass all others in piety, in religion, and that one wisdom which sees that all things are governed and directed by the will of the immortal gods."

And from among all the great thinkers of modern times, who have proclaimed a pure theism, — from Erigena to Descartes, Newton, Leibnitz, Locke, let me select one sentence from Lord Bacon. Lord Bacon says: "I had rather believe all the fables in the Legend, and the Talmud, and the Alcoran, than that this universal frame is without a mind. It is true, that a little philosophy inclineth man's mind to atheism, but depth in philosophy bringeth men's minds about to religion; for while the mind of man looketh upon second causes scattered, it may sometimes rest in them and go no further; but when it beholdeth the chain of them confederate and linked together, it must needs fly to Providence and Deity."

Again, I believe in God because this faith is the great spring of human progress. Faith in God gives courage, hope, energy, to men; and the nearer the faith approaches to true theism, the greater is its power to carry men upward and onward. The slave, in his chains, strengthened by this faith, is stronger than his tyrant. It nerves the arm of the patriot, fighting the battles of freedom. When Paul crossed the blue Ægean, carrying faith in one living God to Europe, he inspired a new life in the decaying mass of the Roman empire, and founded modern civilization. When Mohammed taught his wild Arab tribes to renounce idolatry, and accept one God, he created the seeds of a civilization which illuminated Europe for many hundred years. When Luther defied Rome, in the name of a faith purified from its corruptions, and Gustavus Adolphus died fighting for freedom of spirit, they planted the germs of modern art, science, literature. When the Puritans fought at Naseby, under Cromwell, and when they founded New England, for the sake of a reformed reformation, they gave a stimulus to human civilization and human progress which has not yet ceased to operate in Europe and America. All nations which have made progress in art, literature, science, or social life, have been inspired with a faith, more or less clear, in the invisible and eternal. Let atheism, or semi-atheism, or a low, superstitious theism prevail; and human life goes backward. Let faith revive; society becomes pure, strong, and progressive.

And, lastly, I believe in God, because this faith is needed for the peace, comfort, happiness of individual man. I received, not long ago, from some friend, a pamphlet defending atheism and attacking religion with a certain blind zeal, which is almost pathetic. When I hear such words, I say, "Father, forgive them: they know not what they do." The atheist looks through the universe, and finds no God. He searches the furthest nebula, and God is not there. He examines the structure of the human body, and finds no trace of the divine hand. He interrogates the past, and it is silent; he demands of the future, and it has no voice. The universe is a great dead machine, clashing on and on; coming from nowhere, going nowhere; made for no end, inspired by no wisdom, filled with no love. Man is the child of chance and clay, made of a few chemical elements, to be dissolved into them again. I ask him, "What shall I live for?" He replies, "I do not know. Live for what you please. Eat, drink, and die." The oppressed cry out to God to help them; but the atheist tells them, there is no God to hear their cry. The poor, the sick, the wretched, the lonely, are happy because they have faith in God. The atheist takes away this last support of the miserable, this last restraint on the powerful, this foundation of justice between man and man, this terror to evil-doers, this strength of the upright, — he takes it away, and says, "Die like the brutes, in your darkness and despair." But no: he cannot take it away. Man is made to believe; and the belief in God rests on surer grounds than logic or demonstration; namely, on human nature itself. Some truths are self-evident as soon as men look at them: they need no argument, and cannot be demonstrated. So Proclus says, "He who thinks that all things can be demonstrated takes away demonstration itself;" and Epictetus declares, that "Whoever denies self-evident truths cannot be reasoned with, for he has no intellectual modesty."

We have now come to the end of our brief survey of the first division of our subject; namely, of the questions between the atheists and the theists. We have found that it is difficult if not impossible, to demonstrate the existence of God; and as difficult, if not impossible, not to believe in God. Ninety-nine men out of a hundred, on the surface of the earth, believe in God or Gods, outside of the world and above it, who are more powerful, and more wise than man. Most of those who deny the existence of God, deny the name rather than the thing. They substitute for God Nature, or the Soul of the World, or the Nexus of Laws by which the universe is governed. But they are obliged to attribute to this Web of Laws, or to Nature, the power of evolving, out of itself, order, beauty, adaptation of parts to parts, life, growth, intellect, will. As nothing can come from nothing, all this must have been present implicitly in the Kosmos, before it was evolved explicitly. Consequently, they believe in an infinite Kosmos, containing all the intelligence, power, wisdom, law now extant, and capable of producing it all; that is, they believe in an infinite Creator. The only difference between such atheists and theists is, that the atheist supposes his Supreme Being to produce intelligent results without intelligence, and unconsciously; the theist believes him to produce them intelligently and consciously.

The being of God cannot be demonstrated, because the idea of God is the unity of all necessary ideas, —

the coming together into one of the ideas of necessary being, perfection, cause, intelligence, right, beauty, infinity, and personal will. Now, as each of these ideas is a necessary idea, and cannot be explained out of any thing more simple than itself (which is essential to a proof), all of these taken together cannot be explained out of any thing more simple. Consequently, God's existence cannot be proved, as against one disposed to deny it. But this is no misfortune; for in this respect belief in God stands on the same basis as belief in our own existence, and in that of the outward universe. Neither of these can be proved. They are not believed on the ground of argument, but are known experimentally. I know my own existence, through consciousness, by a mental experience. I know the outward universe, through observation, by the experience of the senses. We commune with ourselves through consciousness: we commune with nature, through the senses. From this communion results our knowledge of each. We know God in the same way, just as far as we commune with him outwardly and inwardly. When we look through nature, and see, back of its changing events an unchanging Cause, under its finite phenomena an infinite Substance, and behind its manifold adaptations an intelligent design, — we come into communion with God through nature. When we look within, and, behind our wrong being and doing, find the conception of a perfect right; behind our lukewarm affections, the idea of a perfect love; and behind our sorrows and weakness, the undying hope of a perfect peace, — we commune with God inwardly. All knowledge comes from communion or intercourse; that is, action and reaction. We cannot know any thing passively. Knowledge arises from life. The knowledge of the outward world comes from sensible experience, or living contact of the senses, by action and reaction. Knowledge of ourselves comes from conscious experience, by looking in upon ourselves, and setting the soul into a living activity. And so knowledge of God does not come passively to any man; but only as he communes, by an active spiritual experience, with God; or, as the Bible says, "Spiritual things must be spiritually discerned."

SECOND STEP.

FROM THEISM TO CHRISTIANITY.

"In the guise of human natures,
Folded round his deep heart now,
Manhood gracious in his features,
Godhood glorious on his brow."

JULIA WARD HOWE.

CHAPTER I.

The Historic Christ.

WE have taken the first step of belief, in rising from atheism to theism. The second step is from theism to Christianity. And here we encounter a new class of opponents. Hitherto we have been dealing with materialists and atheists, with those who deny the spirituality of man, and who reduce God to a force, tied to matter. But now we encounter those who, believing firmly in spirit and in God, deny that Christianity is any advance beyond theism.

This class of theists have, in this country, given the name of "Free Religion" to their system of belief. They constitute a body of able and earnest thinkers, whose views Christian believers cannot afford to neglect. In this division of our argument we shall, first, meet their critical objections against historic Christianity; secondly, their metaphysical objections against the theory of Christianity; thirdly, we shall show wherein Christianity is an advance on pure theism; and, lastly, we will consider some special objections to Christian facts or doctrines.

Before proceeding to notice the objections brought against Christianity by Free Religion, we may properly ask what are the ascertained facts concerning Christ? What historic certainties are there on which we may base any after theories? What do we know about Christ?

Strictly speaking, we cannot be said to *know* any historic fact. We have seen, in a previous chapter, that all history is made up of probabilities. But these probabilities sometimes approach so near the limits of certainty as to amount practically to knowledge. We may, very properly, speak of knowing the fact of the existence of Washington, Napoleon, or Julius Cæsar. In this popular sense, therefore, we ask, What do we know about Christ and Christianity?

First, we know that there is such a fact as Christianity. Christianity is one of the great religions of the world. It is the religion of Europe and America; only slightly to be found in Asia or Africa. It is the religion associated with the highest form of human civilization, the most advanced and advancing culture, and the best morality. It is the religion of the most enlightened and powerful nations. If you wish to know the latest discoveries in chemistry, astronomy, or geology, you do not go to Hindoo, Chinese, or Mohammedan *savans*, but to the scholars of Christendom. If you wish to see the best works of art, either pictures or statues; or to read the best books, the deepest philosophy, the noblest poetry,— you still go to Christendom, not to the Mongols or the Arabs. If you wish to know the history or geography of the earth, you must have recourse to European libraries, maps, and globes. The commerce of the globe is in Christian hands; and the sails which whiten the five oceans are surmounted by the flag of some Christian nation. Christendom contains the power of the world. Its armies, navies, science, literature, art, governments, manufactures, mechanism, commerce, agriculture, are incomparably before those of all the other races of mankind; and Christendom is advancing, while they are stationary or retrograde.

We do not say that the civilization of Christendom is the result of Christianity alone. But that Christianity has something to do with it appears from the fact of the close association of the religion and the civilization. There is some manifest affinity between the two. A common civilization is found among the five Aryan races who profess a common religion. The two Asiatic members of this family, which are not Christian, do not share in this civilization. It is not therefore the result of race; for the Persians and Hindoos belong to the same ethnological family with the Greeks, Latins, Celts, Germans, and Slavi. It is not the result of climate, soil, or other geographical conditions. These were the same in Germany, Norway, England, and Russia a thousand years ago as they are to-day; but no civilization arose in those regions until their inhabitants were converted to Christianity.

Christianity has been the religion of Christendom for at least fifteen centuries. Under Constantine, in the year 325, it became the religion of Rome. It then was so powerful a faith that it conquered the Roman empire. Where did it come from? Such an effect must have a cause. What was its cause? What created Christianity?

Go back another century, — a hundred years before Constantine. We still find Christianity as a wide extended faith, in Europe, Asia, and Africa; with its bishops, its theologians, its churches, its rites and ceremonies, its great writers, its numerous books. But especially it had its Sacred Book; its New Testament, containing the four Gospels, the Book of Acts, and the Epistles, — nearly, if not quite, the same books which we have now. This New Testament we find in Asia, Africa, and Europe. Irenæus — who lived in Gaul, at Lyons, about A.D. 180, and wrote before A.D. 200 — was a disciple of Polycarp, who was a disciple of John. He quotes largely from Matthew, Mark, Luke, and John; calling the Gospels by these names. Away in this western part of Europe, they then read the same four Gospels which we read now. And about the same time Tertullian in Carthage, in Western Africa, was quoting the same books. And Clement in Alexandria was doing the same. And Origen, after him, did the same. Therefore we find this story of Jesus Christ, which we now read and believe, was read and believed by Christian churches in all parts of the civilized world seventeen hundred years ago. Now go back two hundred years further, and what can we discover concerning Christianity? Nothing. There was no Christianity in the world. The reign of Augustus has sent down to us a great number of works by the best authors. It was an era of intellectual light. If Christianity had existed before or during that period, we should have heard of it from Cicero, Horace, Virgil, Ovid, Sallust, or Livy. There is no trace of it: it did not exist in the age of Augustus; and one hundred and fifty years later it is in every part of the Roman empire, and all these churches point back to Judæa as the origin of their faith; all say it comes from Jesus of Nazareth. From all the churches of Gaul, Italy, Greece, Carthage, Alexandria, Antioch, Asia, in the second century, lines converge towards Galilee and Jerusalem at the beginning of the first. It is as when you see in the sky rays of light converging from every side toward a dark cloud. You say, at once, that the sun is behind the cloud at the point where they seem to come together. By the same reasoning, we say Christianity must have begun in Galilee and Judæa, toward the beginning of the first century.

Christianity must have had its commencement and its cause. Its commencement, we have seen, must have been, just about the time when the New Testament reports Jesus to have lived, and just in the same place. All the churches, all Christendom, have declared their faith to have come from him, and to be contained in these books. This is the reason for believing in Jesus as the Founder of Christianity; and for believing that his life and teachings are contained, substantially, in the four Gospels: we believe it for the same reason that we believe any other fact of history, — because all the testimony is that way. History rests on faith in human testimony. Take away that faith, and no history would be possible. Now we have seen, that Christianity, as an immense phenomenon in human history, must have had a cause; that it must have commenced in Judæa in the time of Jesus; that all the testimony of all the Christian churches, is that Jesus is its Founder; and that his life is in the New Testament. If you do not accept such testimony, you have no ground for believing in any historical fact at all, and history ceases to exist.

Why, for example, do we believe in the existence and wonderful career of Alexander the Great, who, finding himself at the age of twenty, king of a small country, marched to the conquest of Asia with 35,000 men, — about the number contained in one of our army *corps*, — conquered Asia Minor; defeated half a million of Persian troops at Issus; took Tyre; conquered Egypt; defeated another army of a million men at Arbela; entered Babylon, Susa, and Persepolis; conquered all Persia; crossed the snow mountains into Bactria; entered India, and defeated King Porus there; and having established a mighty empire, and altered permanently the course of human events, died at the age of thirty-two years? Why do we believe such a marvellous story as this? We have no account of his life from any contemporary writer: Arrian, Plutarch, Diodorus Siculus, and Quintus Curtius,— his four Evangelists,— all lived three centuries after him. But his life and career stand solidly in history, accepted by all. Why? Because the testimony we have, is all that way; and because other events of the age fit into it. For the same reason, we believe in the life of Jesus,— only, in his case we have also the testimony of eye-witnesses and contemporaries.

Since Christianity began in Palestine, among the Jews, and somewhere about the beginning of the first century, it must have begun in one of two ways,— either by the teaching of a single great prophet, or by a gradual development out of previous religions. Religions have commenced in both ways. Some great religions have no authors, but have grown up out of the spirit of their nation and age. Such were Brahminism, and the religions of ancient Egypt, Greece, Rome, and Scandinavia. But others have had single great prophets for their founders; as those of Moses, Confucius, Zoroaster, Mohammed, Buddha. The first class of religions are developed very slowly; the second class come suddenly, in a single generation. Christianity arose suddenly, within a very short period; therefore it must have belonged to the second class, and have had a prophet for its author.

That the account of Jesus in the four Gospels is

substantially correct, appears from the nature of the narrative and the narrators. A consistent picture of his character rises in our minds as we read the Gospels, composed of the traits which they contain. But these Gospels are put together without any method; with no biographical art. The Evangelists simply remember: they do not compose. They seem to have made themselves into so many mirrors placed around Jesus, to reflect his actions and words down through the ages. If you place four mirrors around a statue, each will contain something which the others have, and something which they have not. So the Evangelists, each adding some original traits to the picture, contain also repetitions of each other's story. It does not appear that they themselves understood the character they are describing, or the motives of his actions. They are evidently filled with awe, love, and admiration for Jesus; but they never undertake to admire, or to describe his character. Still less do they enter upon any critical investigation of his ideas, his purpose, or the meaning of his career. They photograph his life as the sun photographs a picture. A photograph may be imperfect, may be blotched and obscure in this and that part; but it is faithful. Every thing in it means something which was really in the original. If the Evangelists had been asked to write a biography of Jesus, in the style of Strauss, Renan, or Neander, — defending this fact, accounting for that, and explaining away the other, and so making a portrait of Jesus according to their own philosophy, — they could not have done it. They did not understand him enough, to invent any part of the story. They can narrate honestly, simply, sometimes perhaps erroneously, what they saw and heard: that is their whole power. If they are inspired writers, their historic inspiration is that which comes from love. They loved their Master so, that all he said, and all he did, was precious to their hearts. So a mother's love for her child leads her to remember all his little speeches, all his little ways. There is no memory like that of the lover, on the living tablets of whose heart are imperishably stamped all the looks, the smiles, the words of the idol of his dreams. What Mary is reported to have done, that the Evangelists did with their Master's life: they "hid these things in their heart."

It is clear that such writers as these could never have invented the character they have given us. How could they have conceived a character which, it is evident, they do not understand themselves in their own report of it? And how could four writers conspire to invent such a character, and then communicate it in broken inartistic fragments, which must be carefully arranged, and put together by successive generations of critics, and from which, thus put together, there finally emerges the greatest Personage of all time?

If, then, we find a unity in the character of Jesus, thus represented, it is evidently human and historical. It is because he really lived and moved before the eyes of these inartistic, unpractised narrators. They give us all they saw and all they heard, with no attempt at consistency, no explanation of any apparent contradictions. They make themselves wholly into eye, ear, and tongue. They see, hear, and tell: that is all.

Do we then find a unity in the character so described? and, if so, what is it?

Jesus first appears as a Reformer of a very radical character, and yet attaching himself firmly to the past, — holding fast to its vital faith, but rejecting its traditions. In the sermon on the mount, in which are brought together, apparently, his earliest discourses, he gives a new interpretation to the Mosaic law; a new view of the kingdom of heaven, or reign of the Messiah; of alms-giving, prayer, and fasting; of the providence of God; and of the essence of goodness. And yet he declares, that he has not come to destroy the law, that he has come to fulfil, not to destroy. To fulfil, here means to carry forward to a fuller perfection. The letter shall not pass until its spirit is taken up into a higher form. This is already something very unusual. A prophet is commonly a one-sided man, possessed by his idea, hurried away by his deep conviction of one truth, or his horror of one evil. He does not stop to limit or qualify: if he did, his power would be gone. He must commonly overstate and be extravagant, or he does not say all he feels. But Jesus never overstated, never was extravagant, and yet spoke with overcoming authority. Jesus was radical and conservative in one. Let us see the facts which show this to be so.

From one point of view, we may say that Jesus was the greatest Radical that ever lived. He set aside all forms, not impatiently or violently, but as easily as a grown man puts aside the foolish notions of a child. The sabbath was only sacred to him as it helped man. We are not as free to-day in our treatment of Sunday, as he was in treating the sabbath of his time. He healed the sick, took walks in the fields with his disciples, and did many things which it was not lawful to do. In regard to clean and unclean meats, distinguished so painfully in the books of Moses, he said that a man was not defiled by the meat which went into his mouth, but by the words which came out of it. People still call a church the "house of God," as though God were in some way specially present in it. But Jesus told the woman of Samaria, that not this place nor that place is a place of worship; but that the pure heart is the only house of God and gate of heaven.

He had nothing of the conventional prophet about him. He did not make himself a saint by living in a cell, eating roots, and wearing sackcloth. He came eating and drinking like others; he went among all sorts of people, — old men and little children, Samaritans and Phœnicians, Roman soldiers and the unpopular tax-gatherers, the honest and pure, the soiled and stained. All this was new and strange; but he does not lay stress on it himself, or call attention to it, or proclaim it as a discovery of his own. He does it as simply and naturally as if there were nothing new in it. But his ideas were more radical than his manners. Judaism was a law, a system of rules; its God a Law-giver and Law-avenger, Judge, and King. Jesus did away with law and rule, writing the law in the heart. To say your prayers, is not to pray; to repeat words, is not to pray. He gives no command to pray at all; but only says, "When thou prayest," let it be in secret, talking alone with God, without many words; for God hears you before you begin; saying what you really feel, not what you think you ought to feel; and in faith, speaking to God, as sure that he hears you and will help you as when you go to your neighbor's house to ask him to help you lift a stone which is too heavy for you to raise alone. To murder a man is not merely to stab him with a knife, or beat him with a club. It is to stab him with a bitter word, to bruise his heart with an unkind suspicion. Licentiousness is in the ungoverned desire, the indulged imagination, the irregular thought. To fast, is not to look sad, and to make a merit of abstinence; it is not to parade our sacrifices. But it is to give up what we like, and say nothing about it; to make sacrifices, and be happy in doing it, cheerful givers for the sake of God and man. Truth is not in keeping one's oath or promise: truth is in having our words in exact correspondence to our thought; without promising at all, to be simply sincere. Goodness is not in loving and helping good people and agreeable people; but in finding something good, something to love, in every one.

For God is not law and Law-giver, King and Judge, chiefly; but Friend, blessed Friend, to all his creatures. He does not love the good, and hate the evil: he sends soft rain and heavenly sunlight to comfort the sinner's heart. He is not above nature only, as an awful power; but in every flower that blushes in its beauty by the meadow stream, in every star that flames on the midnight sky. Every little bird that droops and dies in its nest falls as softly into God's hand as do his saints and martyrs. Little things which we despise, God prizes, counting every hair of our heads. Goodness is not in talk or profession, but in action. He does not follow me, says Jesus, who cries Lord! Lord! the loudest; but he who does, not my will, but my Father's will most truly. The man who rudely and impiously says to God, "I will not obey," but then repents and obeys, is better than the man of solemn piety, who says all holy things, and then forgets to do them.

How radical is all this! How this subsoil plough goes under the roots of all popular, fashionable religion in Christ's day, and perhaps in ours too. Is it not curious that his rebuke seems to strike us as squarely here in America now, as it did his neighbors in Nazareth and Cana then?

The Judaism in which Jesus had been educated was a law, a system of rules. He teaches that rules are nothing, but the spirit every thing. Judaism was the worship of an all-holy, all-powerful Judge and King above the world; rewarding the good, punishing the evil. Jesus taught a Father, who sees his prodigal child a great way off; who sends blessings, not wrath, on sinners; and is more glad when the naughty child comes back, than he is because the good boys and girls are behaving well. Judaism, finally, was an intense nationality, a narrow bigoted belief in one people, as the special favorite of God. Jesus taught a kingdom of heaven to which the poor in spirit, and the meek, and the pure of heart, should belong, all of right. He said that many should come from the east and west and sit down with Abraham and Isaac, when the Jews should be cast out; that God's house would be filled by those taken from the by-ways and the hedges. He taught that the heathen who had never heard of Judaism or Christianity, would find at the last day that they were Christians without knowing it, when they fed the hungry, clothed the naked, visited the sick, and were kind to the stranger. So independent was Jesus of the Judaism around him; so radical in his reform of its traditions!

And yet he could say, as we have seen, that he did not come to destroy the law and the prophets, but to fulfil them. He did not break with the past: he recognized the law of growth by which the stalk comes from the seed, the blossom from the stalk, the fruit from the blossom. So he remained a Jew, went to the Jewish feasts, worshipped in the Jewish Temple, and accepted the part of the Jewish Messiah. He took the old forms, and filled them full of a higher meaning. Thus the boldest radicalism would have been the best conservatism, had the Jewish people consented. Had they taken him as their true King, he would have made them the leaders of the human race. For he would have preserved the whole spirit of Judaism, while dropping its letter. Its forms, which separated them from mankind, would have disappeared. But the noble spirit of Judaism, — its faith in one supreme and living God, making all men brethren, as the Jews were brothers, — this would have been the atoning principle to unite all men together.

This was the vast idea of Jesus. In this sense he understood himself to be the Messiah foreordained from the foundation of the world. Before Abraham was, he was the Christ of God; a King, born and sent into the world to bear witness to the truth. In him culminated the long preparations of history. He was the Heir of all things; and in him, as the Centre of humanity, all the races, religions, and civilizations of the earth were to be made one. This was his great aim, — the highest object which the human mind can conceive. The fact that he claimed to be the Christ and Son of God; his including among his subjects all who loved the truth, and obeyed it; and his expectation that there should be but one fold and one Shepherd, — these prove that the universal human leadership of the race was the mission he had accepted as his own.

Thus far all is historical and all human. But now we must take another step. To believe one's self the leader of the human race, and to be so, are two different things. To be the leader of a single race, a single nation, during a single period, — it is only necessary to be fully possessed with the ideas of that race, nation, and period. But to lead the human race as its religious Guide, it is necessary to be universal, to omit nothing, to embody all the essential ideas of human religion. Did Jesus do this? This is what Free Religion denies, and Christianity asserts. Free Religion considers Jesus as one great Teacher, perhaps the greatest; but to be passed by at last, and left behind; possibly, already passed by. But Christianity accepts Jesus as Son of God and Son of man; perfect man in his character, fulfilling the idea of man; also perfect manifestation of God, showing to men their Heavenly Father perfectly, — "the image of the invisible God," and the First-born (or Chief) of the whole creation. According to this view, he is never to be left behind, but to grow more and more into the love and faith of the world, until he has united the human race in one brotherhood. He is to reign till he has subdued all enemies under him; and then he is to deliver up the kingdom to God, even the Father.

Free Religion denies that any one man can be all this; because to be this implies perfection of nature, and all men are imperfect. But in denying that any man can be perfect, Free Religion seems to be yet hampered by the fatal doctrine of hereditary and entire depravity. Why should not one man be perfect? Is sin so natural to man, that perfection is unnatural? Were we made to be sinners, made to be always wrong? Many men have approached a spotless perfection; why should not one man have attained it? We are, all of us, perfectly good at some moments in our lives, when we submit wholly to truth and love, — why should not one man have been always in this state of entire submission and entire love? Jesus had no such doubt. He did not believe that man was necessarily imperfect: he became perfect, in order to be the Author of the same perfection to all who obey him. He said to the average men about him, neither better nor worse than we are, "Be perfect, even as your Father in heaven is perfect."

But when we claim perfection for Jesus, what do we mean? Not divine perfection, but human. To be perfect, is to be entire and absolute in the human order as God is in the divine order. When we say that Jesus was the one perfect Being, we do not make of him a faultless monster, nor take him out of the human and historic order. What we say is, that he fulfilled the intention of God concerning man, and became purely and wholly a man; and thus showed to us that we can

8

do the same. He showed that sin is unnatural, not natural; that we are not so tied and bound by weakness and evil, that we cannot love God and man. Since Christ has succeeded in this, we can succeed too. This subject we shall pursue in our next chapter.

The perfection of Jesus was moral perfection. It consisted in this, that he lived always in communion with God, as we live sometimes; that he lived always in the spirit of unselfish love, as we live sometimes; that his inspiration was constant, while ours is transient. So he, in the providence of God, was made and became the Leader of the human race, the Inspirer of faith in God, the Atonement to unite all in one.

The one great outward proof that Jesus was thus the Christ of humanity, the ordained Leader of the human race to God and to each other, is found in his resurrection. This is the only miracle on which the apostles lay stress as evidence of his mission. Paul does not mention the other miracles in his speeches or letters, but he dwells constantly on the resurrection of Jesus. When Jesus appeared to die, he did not die: he remained alive. When he seemed to go down, he did not go down: he went up. When he seemed to go away, he did not go away: he remained. The "power of the resurrection" is, that it shows us a living, ever-present Christ, with his church, coming back to us, coming to reign more and more. The miracle of the resurrection is not a violation of the laws of nature, but an unveiling of the higher law of life. It shows us in death a going up, not a going down; a coming near, not a going away; a fulness of immor tality.

The objections to this view are chiefly *a priori* and metaphysical. Theodore Parker believes that Christ was imperfect, — not that he sees any special imperfection in him, but because all men are imperfect, and must be so. All men, no doubt, are finite. No one can have infinite perfection. But, unless we believe in original sin, why shall not man attain to finite perfection, to the perfection of human nature? Why may not Jesus, in the providence of God, — prepared by organization, educated by the great history and traditions of his people, — have reached this point, and become the perfect man, who reconciles religion and morality, faith and works, love to God and love to man, and is filled with that divine life which will at last bring together all races and all religions into a perfect brotherhood? As far as I can see, the principal objection in the way is the belief in natural depravity, — the belief that all men must be imperfect, and that therefore Jesus must have been so.

Those who do not accept a necessary depravity may believe in Jesus, not as one among many past prophets and teachers, who did their work, and then went to their graves; but as the ever-living, ever-present, inspiring, and saving Friend of man. We may believe in him, as the one who liveth and was dead, and behold he is alive for evermore. His life, death, and resurrection are the hope and strength of the world. He is and remains our King. Because he was faithful in all things, he became perfect, and is able to make us so. He is to reign till he subdues all things under him, by the power of his truth and his love. All this is a part of history. He is not the less human, as we shall see in the next chapter, for being so perfect, but the more so. For man was made to be perfect. Jesus, our Brother, went before us, in the high providence of God, leading the way upward from earth to heaven. The more we believe in him, the stronger and better we are.

The power of Christ and of Christianity consists in this immense hope for man. Jesus saw all the sin, all the ignorance, all the weakness of man, and yet hoped for him. He foresaw the denial of Peter, the betrayal of Judas, saw that all his disciples should forsake him in his hour of trial; and yet he had no doubt that they were all to be one with him, as he was one with God. The divine character of the great prayer in the seventeenth chapter of John, is, that it is filled full of this absolute, unwavering hope. About to die, forsaken and alone, he yet says that God has given him power over all flesh, to give them eternal life. He calls on God to glorify him with the glory he had with him before the world was. He was so sure of the faith of his disciples, that he prayed for them in the full conviction that they belonged to him and to God, and were not of the world: he prayed that he and they might be one in God. He told his disciples that he was to return to them after death, and remain with them; that he was "to be with them always, even to the end of the world." He told them to go into all the earth, and preach the gospel to every creature. Filled with so great a faith in God and man, sure that man was to become one with God, and that all discord, sin, woe, wickedness, were to cease, — he went to die, attended by this shining light, and left this great hope as the inspiration for all time.

And now we ask, has Jesus been outgrown? In these eighteen centuries, has he been left behind, in any one particular, by the advancing race of man? Is he not still our Leader, Chief, and Friend; the best Friend we have, our Brother, Teacher, and Master? Without him, and his religion, what satisfaction is there in life, what hope in death, what comfort in sorrow, what strength in our weakness, what light in our darkness?

CHAPTER II.

Nothing Unnatural in Christ or in Christianity.

THE object of this chapter is to show that there is nothing unnatural in Christianity. Christianity has hitherto been opposed to rational theism by definitions which have given to it an unnatural character. Christ has been assumed to stand outside of nature and history. His religion has been called supernatural in a sense which made it seem unnatural. In regard to Jesus Christ himself, we find two distinct and seemingly opposite views prevailing at the present time. The first is the traditional and general opinion that he was not like other men in his person, his endowments, his work, or his character; that his person was superhuman, his endowments supernatural, his work miraculous, and his character intellectually infallible and morally impeccable; that he was a miraculous creation, that he was divinely inspired and sent, that he did not sin, did not err, will never be superseded, and is the Master, Lord, King of the human race for ever. Hence it is assumed that he was not a man only and purely, but something more.

The other view is that which has been becoming more and more popular since the days of Theodore Parker, not only in this country, but also in England, France, and Germany. It is, that Jesus was a man like all other men, born like other men, formed by circumstances as other men are formed, partaking of the errors of his age, not supernatural, but wholly natural; working no miracles, not infallible, but falling into errors; not perfect morally; capable of being superseded and outgrown; and, in short, purely a man, like other men.

It will be observed that these two theories, so utterly opposite, nevertheless agree in one assumption. Both assume that perfection is unnatural to man; that man is necessarily imperfect, mentally and morally; that to be sinless is unnatural; that to see truth so clearly as to be certain of it and not liable to be mistaken, is unnatural: in other words, that it is not natural for man to be good, and that a perfectly good man is necessarily a supernatural, or (what is thought the same thing) an unnatural being.

The one class of thinkers say, "Jesus was sinless and infallible, and worked miracles, therefore he was superhuman." The others say, " He was human, and therefore he could not work miracles or be perfect." The first class, wishing to believe in the superiority of Jesus, think it necessary to believe him superhuman; the other class, not wishing to believe him superhuman, think it necessary to deny his superiority. Both classes agree that any such inward superiority as is ascribed to Jesus in the New Testament, implies a superhuman element. That is, again, both classes assume the essential poverty of human nature.

But why may we not suppose that man's nature is higher than either party believes? What if man was made to be all Jesus was; what if human nature is not necessarily sinful, but otherwise; what if sin and error are unnatural, not natural: then it may follow that Jesus did all that he is claimed to have done in the Gospels; that he is all that he is described to have been, and yet instead of being at all unnatural, is a truer and more perfectly natural man than any other has been. Perhaps the greatness of Jesus may have been just here, — that he was the man of men, the truest man, fulfilling the type of humanity. Perhaps the great lesson of his life is, that human nature is not essentially evil, but good. Perhaps his mission was to show us one perfect specimen of the human race; one ideal pattern; one such as all are hereafter to become.

If this view be correct, then it may reconcile the war between the Naturalists and Supernaturalists.

The Naturalists can then accept the leading facts in the life of Jesus, and yet believe in him as a purely human being. The Supernaturalists can believe in his perfect holiness, wisdom, and power, and yet not deny his simple humanity. I propose, therefore, to adduce some facts which show that there is nothing claimed in the Gospels for Christ which is inconsistent with the assumption of his being made in all respects like his brethren.

I do not consider the question of his supernatural birth; first, because it rests on a different kind of evidence from the other facts of the life of Jesus, of a much more legendary character; secondly, because it is difficult to know exactly what is intended by the narrative; thirdly, because, whatever it may mean, it cannot imply that Jesus was not a man, made in all respects like his brethren. I am willing, as a Supernaturalist, to consider this whole narration as legendary, not having the historic stamp of the rest of the Gospels.

I will begin with Jesus on the purely human side; claiming for him nothing exceptional in his nature or birth. I will admit that his character resulted, like that of all other men, from these three factors, — organization, education, and free choice.

How much of goodness, then, may he have inherited without being superhuman?

We see some children born good. They seem to have escaped, to a very great degree, the innate tendencies to evil which others suffer from. A confluence of compensating influences neutralizes the evil in their organization. It may happen that opposite faults in parents will result in a balanced, well-proportioned organization in the child. At all events we know it to be a fact, that the child of parents who have grave faults of character is often born free from them all. Can we not, therefore, believe that in occasional instances, there may be a child born in whom all these depraved tendencies neutralize each other, and allow the infant to begin with a nature like that of the primal man, — liable indeed to sin, but capable of escaping sin. This is all that we need assume concerning the birth of Jesus; and there is nothing in this which is superhuman.

The second source of character is education; under which term we include all influences, outward and inward. Now, we see many cases of children who grow up under influences peculiarly favorable to goodness, — influences which tend not to deprave, but to elevate. We all know of homes, where the usual atmosphere is pure, where life goes on temperately and serenely; where conscience and truth are domesticated; where love makes the heart happy, and warms the household intercourse with its tender fire. It is only necessary to suppose Jesus to have grown up in such a sphere as this. The natural, simple piety of his Nazarene home, the motherly love of Mary, the innocence of that country life, the influence of that beautiful natural scenery, the teachings of great prophetic masters, whose works made his library, the expectation of the Messiah, — these were the natural, not supernatural, influences which came to Jesus to make his education, and to a genius like his they were sufficient.

Then there were also given divine influences, — influences which come to all, — to lift the soul of the child into a higher insight. God is not far from any one of us. We all receive influences from him. It is only necessary to believe that Jesus received a higher measure of that Holy Spirit than most men; that the divine Providence which gives to all men a special mission, gave him his, and that he received a full and constant current of inspiration into his soul. Consider the difference between the mathematical gifts of common men and those of Sir Isaac Newton; between the organizing gifts of common men and those of a Hannibal or a Napoleon; between the poetic gifts of common men and those of a Dante or a Shakspeare; between the artistic gifts of common men and those of a Mozart or a Raffaelle. There is nothing superhuman in such extraordinary endowments. Why, then, doubt that God may have conferred on Jesus a like moral and spiritual superiority to all other men, making him the spiritual Master of the race, as these are its masters in science, poetry, war, and art.

But to satisfy the faith of the church, we must go farther than this. We must accept the fact of the moral integrity of Jesus; that Jesus was sinless; that he was perfectly pure from evil from the first, and all the way through. And this is said to be unnatural, — superhuman. But why? Was man made to be a sinner, or to be free from sin? Did not God intend us to be sinless? Does not even orthodoxy confess that God made man naturally good? Does not our conscience condemn us for every act of sin? And is not that a proof, in our very nature, that we are not compelled to sin? Jesus himself does not consider his own perfection as exceptional, but calls on all men to be like him in this matter: "Be ye therefore perfect," he says, "as your Father in heaven is perfect."

Nevertheless, it may be said, it is not possible that Jesus, or any one else, should be morally perfect, since all experience shows that every one has his faults and his moral defects. But does it follow that because the great multitude of any class of beings fail to reach the perfection of their class, that no one shall ever reach it? Is it not more probable that, amid this universal aspiration and tendency, one may at last succeed? Every plant has its typical form. Among ten thousand plants, not one perhaps reaches it; but may not one somewhere arrive? The typical form of an elm-tree is of a perfectly symmetrical series of curves, in which every limb curves upward, and then bends over, and then falls in a trailing sweep of innumerable lace-like threads of greenery. Out of a thousand elms, not one attains this perfect symmetry. Some few almost reach it; but do you say, because you have never found a perfect elm, that it is unnatural for an elm to be symmetrical? No, you say just otherwise. The true nature of the elm is to be found in this tendency toward perfection; and if, at last, an elm should be discovered with every limb, branch, twig, and leaf in perfect proportion, you would not call it unnatural, but the final attainment and fulfilment of its nature. So, if somewhere in the long reaches of human history, amid all its sin and shame, its hard routine, its distortion, its bitterness, its falsehood, one man shall appear without stain; always tender, always strong, giving his life for his race; full of faith in God, full of hope for man; without disguise; without pretence; one on whose pure life the attempt to find a spot results in a hypercriticism so small as to be simply ridiculous, — then shall we say that such a man is unnatural and superhuman, and not rather that he is more human than any one else; the man God meant all men to be; the one who reveals to us what our nature really is; what it is really capable of; what it is one day to become?

"But," says the Naturalist, "are not all men fallible? and if Jesus is only a man, could he be infallible: must he not have fallen into error?" "To err is human;" therefore, if Jesus was human, must he not have erred?

That the knowledge of Jesus was limited; that he did not know all sciences and arts which are now known, no one would think of denying. He was not sent to teach astronomy or geology, and so he did not know them. He even says, that, concerning the time of his own triumphant coming, he is ignorant: "Of that day and hour knoweth no man, no not the Son, but the Father only." But that he made mistakes in those things which he professed to know, is another matter, and this I do not believe. In all his teaching concerning God, man, duty, immortality, no mistake has been, or is likely to be, pointed out; for here he spoke from knowledge, not theory. These were the things he saw by the intuition of his soul, so he knew them. And in this also he was not superhuman; for this is true of all men. All men are certain of that which they really know. If there is such a thing as knowledge, then, so far as it goes, it excludes the possibility of error. A mathematician is perfectly sure of the laws of mathematics, so far as they have been discovered and verified. An astronomer is sure of the movements of the heavenly bodies, so far as they have been ascertained and verified. All modern science rests on this word "verification." Whatever has been verified has been made certain, beyond the possibility of error. Now the great teachings of Jesus, concerning God and man, have been verified by the experience of sixty generations of Christian men and women. They have guided them to God; they have rescued them from sin; they have created faith, hope, and love in human hearts; they have conquered the fear of death; they have consoled the sufferers under the burdens of life. These are the spiritual verifications which prove the insight of Jesus to be knowledge.

But the theory of the Supernaturalists goes further, and declares that Jesus was divinely sent to be a teacher of the race; that he had a divine mission.

Does not this make him unnatural, and separate him from human nature? Only if we disbelieve in Providence. If we have faith in a living God, a Father and Friend of man, who does not only interpose once in a while, but is present always in human affairs, then every man is sent to do a work; every man has a mission; a mission determined by his capacities and opportunities; a mission which no one can fulfil but himself, since every man has his proper gift from the Lord. The mission of Jesus differed from that of other men in these two points, — that it was the greatest work ever given to man to do, and that he saw more clearly what it was than other men see theirs.

But was the work of Wesley, for example, an accident? Was the work of Channing undesigned in the providence of God? Did not Martin Luther have a mission? Are not such men sent? Every prophet who has been since the world began, has felt a call to speak, and has gone to do his work often in the heat and bitterness of his spirit, often unwillingly and reluctantly. They hear the call of God in the depths of their souls, and cannot escape. So Jesus heard his call; only, — because his nature was so deep, his spirit so lofty, his mind so clear, his heart so pure, — he heard his great call more distinctly, and knew that God had chosen him among all men to be his true Christ. But neither in this was there any thing unnatural or superhuman.

And when men talk of Christ's work being superseded, we must ask what it is that can be superseded in his work? Can truth ever be superseded or outgrown? Can the time come in which it will not be true that "the pure in heart see God;" that "he who humbles himself shall be exalted"? Will the parables of the Prodigal Son and the Good Samaritan ever be outgrown? Will the Lord's prayer be antiquated? Will the life of Jesus cease to be the illustration of love to God and love to man? What then is to be superseded? Is Christianity to become larger, deeper, purer, higher? Be it so. That is the very event which Jesus predicted, — that the Spirit of Truth should come and lead men into all truth. But whatever higher form religion assumes, it will not abolish Christianity, but only fulfil it, glorify it, and make it more like the ideal in the mind of the Master.

But what shall we say concerning the miracles ascribed to Christ in the Gospels? Are not these, unnatural and superhuman facts false to experience, and opposed to the laws of nature, and so essentially incredible? If I believed these wonderful works of Jesus to be unnatural, if I considered them as violations of law, then I should also say that they were essentially incredible. But believing them, as I do, to be in perfect harmony with law, I consider them neither unnatural, nor opposed to the laws of nature. The electric telegraph or the photograph would have seemed unnatural a hundred years ago. There are mysteries in nature, hidden from the foundation of the world, which are to be revealed hereafter, which would be to us as incredible as the miracles of Jesus seem now.

I believe that Jesus cured sickness with a word and a touch. I believe that he raised the dead. I believe that he rebuked the winds and waves, and fed five thousand men with a few loaves and fishes. I believe in the majority of the wonderful effects upon outward nature ascribed to Jesus in the Gospels, first, because of the historical credibility of these narratives; secondly, because they are simply called "wonderful works," the Evangelists abstaining wholly from any theory concerning their supernatural or other origin; thirdly, because, as Mr. Furness has so well shown, they are the spontaneous outcome of the nature of Jesus, and utterly refused by him when asked for as "signs" or proofs of truth; and, fourthly, because we find analogous facts in human annals showing that such a power is latent in the psychological nature of man. Many have possessed the power of healing diseases by the exercise of will; some have had an instinctive prevision of coming events. Is it not to be expected, then, that when the perfect man arrives, he shall also possess in the most eminent degree this power by which the soul demonstrates its inherent supremacy above the lower forces which govern in the material sphere? These miracles of Jesus were therefore not violations of law, but anticipations of great discoveries to come hereafter. These wonders may appear natural in some future period. A thousand years hence, or ten thousand years hence, they may seem to be as natural as the electric telegraph seems to-day. Jesus did these things not because he was superhuman, but because he was wholly and absolutely human, — the ripe fruit of humanity, the fulness of manhood; and so having his soul *en rapport* with the laws of nature.

Now this view of Christ is the very view taken in the New Testament. All the great qualities, powers, and functions of Jesus are not treated as monopolies, nor as his exclusive possession, but in so many words are spoken of as gifts which he came to impart to other men, therefore as essentially human. Indeed, only thus can he be considered as a mediator. For what is a mediator? A mediator is not one who retains his special gifts, but who is a medium through whom these gifts flow to others. That was the work of Christ. All that he had, all that he was, he communicated to his disciples and through them to the world. Did he work miracles? He says, "Greater works than these shall ye do, because I go to my Father." Was he one with God? He says of his disciples, "That they may be one, even as we are one. I in them, and thou in me." Had the Son of man power on earth to forgive sin? He says to his disciples, "Whosesoever sins ye remit they shall be remitted unto them." Was he perfect? He says, "Be ye perfect." Was he sinless? The Apostle John says, "He who is born of God cannot commit sin." Was

Christ sent to be Judge of the world? Paul says that the saints shall judge the world, and men, and angels. Did Christ "know all things"? The Apostle says, "Ye have an unction from the Holy Ghost, and know all things." Is it said, "In him dwelleth all the fulness of the Godhead, bodily"? The Apostle prays for the Ephesians that ye "may know the love of Christ, which passeth knowledge, that ye may be filled with all the fulness of God." Is it said that "all men shall honor the Son, even as they honor the Father"? Jesus says to his disciples, "He that heareth you, heareth me; and he that despiseth you, despiseth me;" and, "the glory which thou gavest me I have given them." Was Jesus "King and Priest"? It is written that "He hath made us kings and priests unto God." Did he suffer and die for mankind, and so make atonement for them? The Apostle Paul distinctly says, that he himself was "to fill up that which is behind of the afflictions of Christ." Finally, if Jesus was sent to be a Saviour, in any special or peculiar sense, his disciples are sent in the same way; for he says, "As my Father hath sent me, even so send I you." A careful examination of the New Testament will therefore show that Jesus had nothing, and received nothing, which he did not have and receive as a mediator, by communicating all to his disciples, and through them to the human race. We have referred above to passages of the New Testament which declare, *ipsissimis verbis*, that he meant his disciples to receive his power of working miracles, his oneness with God, his power of forgiving sin, his perfectness of character, his office of Judge, his omniscience, his divine fulness, his honor and glory, his kingship and priesthood; and that they should share with him in his atoning work.

It has been objected to Jesus that he taught the doctrine of a devil, and that of demoniacal influence, and so encouraged superstition.

As regards the doctrine of a devil, Jesus speaks of the devil (*Διάβολος*) five times, and of Satan (*Σατανᾶς*) six times. On one of these occasions he calls Peter Satan, "Get thee behind me, Satan," because he had, in kindness and with a good purpose, tempted him to avoid going to Jerusalem to die. This shows that he used the word to personify all temptation. On one occasion he uses the word devil (*Διάβολος*) in the same way, "Have I not chosen you twelve, and one of you is a devil?" He says to the Jews, "Ye are of your father, the devil," where, again, he certainly is not using "devil" in any personal sense, but as meaning the power of evil. It can hardly, therefore, be argued that Jesus has taught the existence of Satan or the devil in the sense since held, as an evil being, the incarnate power of evil and sin, wholly given over to darkness. He uses "devil" as the principle of temptation.

As regards demoniacal possession, I think that Jesus believed in it, and that he spoke to the evil spirits as though they would hear him. A few years ago, I thought that he shared a popular error in this, which this century has outgrown. But within a few years I have been led to believe in the reality of demoniacal possession. I have myself known personally, or by credible testimony, of at least half a dozen instances of persons, who, after having allowed themselves to become spiritual mediums, seem at last to have been taken possession of by a low and unclean order of spirits. And the best way of rescuing them, when they were too far gone to help themselves, was to have some other person possessing greater spiritual force do what Jesus did; namely, order the spirit to go away. I believe that in certain places and periods, the nervous condition of men is such, that the lower order of ghosts may get a control over them, and that when Jesus came, it was just such a time and place as this.

We began by the statement that both Naturalists and Supernaturalists agree that if Christ did what he is reported to have done, and was what the Gospel describes him to have been, he was not a man, but something superhuman. The Naturalists deny that he could be superhuman, and so deny that he did the works. The Supernaturalists, believing and asserting that he did the works, think it necessary to assert also that he was superhuman.

We have seen that we can differ from both, and agree with both. We can agree with the Supernaturalists, that Christ was what the Gospels claim; and agree with the Naturalists, that he was a pure man, and not superhuman. We may differ from both by taking the position that in human nature there is place and room for all the great qualities, powers, and gifts, ascribed to Jesus in the Gospels.

And now, in what sense shall we call Jesus our Lord and Master? Not in any sense which violates the perfect freedom of our thought, and perfect conscientiousness of our actions. But he is our Lord and Master, because "every one that is of the Truth heareth his voice;" because he is the Good Shepherd who goes before the flock, and they follow him; beeause he is the Way, the Truth, and the Life; and because through him we come to the Father, and find God a Father and a Friend. No man's conscience or freedom is violated by taking a master, and receiving with trust his advice and instruction. In fact, no progress is possible for men without such guides. Confidence in our teacher's superior wisdom smooths the way, leads us on, awakens the mind, and develops the soul. All earnest souls seek and find their masters. One man takes Parker, Emerson, and Carlyle, and sits at their feet; another takes Herbert Spencer, Buckle, or Comte. One set of artists never tire of studying the secret of Titian's color, or Michael Angelo's forms. While one class of students feed on Carlyle, he himself lives upon Goethe. As long as Carlyle abode in Goethe, he produced much fruit; but when he left that master, he was cast forth as a branch and was withered. He then "shot Niagara." What would musicians do if they had not their musical masters, — Mendelssohn, Beethoven, Mozart? One person devotes his life to discover "the secret of Hegel;" another to "the secret of Swedenborg." And we may be sure of this, that the only men who will discover and profit by the genius of these masters, are those who study them with faith. Only faith leads to sight. Those who look for faults, find faults, and become fault-finders by profession; but those who look for truth and good, find that. And if, among all these masters, there has been sent one to be a master on the highest theme of all, a teacher in the realm of our highest life, it seems to be a grave mistake to assume toward him the attitude of a critic rather than that of a disciple.

The unquestioned and unquestionable facts which are to be explained, are these: —

1. There is such a phenomenon as Christian faith, which must have come from some source.

2. There are such books as those of the New Testament, which must have had writers.

3. There is such an institution as the Christian Church, which must have had an origin.

That such a person as is described in the Gospels really existed, is admitted by all whose opinions are of any value; such a person in the main. It is admitted that he was a Galilean peasant, of wonderful powers, spiritual, intellectual, and moral; that he was able to rise to the highest point of spiritual and moral insight which man has ever attained; that he went beyond the limitations of Judaism, so as to put the spirit above the letter, and find the essence of the law in love to God and to man. And that his moral and spiritual personality was so deep and high as to constitute the original fountain out of which what we call Christianity took its rise. Other streams have since flowed into the river, but the person of Jesus is its source and origin.

If we deny the existence of such a person as Jesus, we are obliged to assume that his character was an invention by some unknown person or persons, in the first or second century; that the four Gospels were written by these persons, and this wonderful character placed in them, and made to act and live and speak as we find him; placed in connection with historical persons and events and geographical localities; that this invention, undetected, was admitted as a reality; that Christianity sprang out of it; and that, by the middle of the second century, churches were founded on the firm belief in the existence of this person, and contained those who pretended to have seen and talked with his first disciples. And this would have to be believed in order to disbelieve the origin of Christianity from a person; when we know that the great movements of history usually come from persons; that from the personalities of Confucius, Buddha, Zoroaster, Mohammed, Augustine, Plato, Aristotle, Luther, great moral and religious movements have proceeded; and that this is the most usual and natural source of such spiritual phenomena.

Since all phenomena which begin in time must have a cause, the three phenomena of Christian faith, the Christian Church, and the books of the New Testament, must have had a cause; and, among all possible causes, none has any probability, or any evidence in its support, but the personal character of Jesus Christ.

We have endeavored in this chapter to show that there is nothing unnatural, and therefore incredible, in the history of Christ in the New Testament. The facts therein may be historically true, and yet not be opposed to the laws of nature. We will only add, that it is wiser to believe in the possibilities of human nature than to disbelieve in them. It is wiser to believe than to doubt the great concurrent facts of human testimony. It is wise to believe that God's Providence cares for the world, and sends its great teachers and masters. Faith in greatness and goodness is the creative force in the moral world, the power which makes and remakes civilization. It is the source of progress, and so accredits itself as in accordance with the divine laws. Belief in something great, in the past and in the future, is the motive power which carries the world forward, onward, upward.

CHAPTER III.

Christianity an Advance on Theism.

IN maintaining that Christianity is an advance on theism, we are obliged to meet the objections of several very able antagonists, who contend, on their side, that theism is an advance on Christianity. The doctrine usually known as "Religious Radicalism," or as "Free Religion," denies that Christianity is the absolute religion, and regards it as limited, and soon to be superseded and left behind by a more catholic faith. It holds that every thing true and good in Christianity had already been taught by other religions. It asserts that the time has come when Christianity is to be rejected, and that a pure theism is to take its place and do its work.

Some quotations from "The Radical" and "The Index" — periodicals, which are published in the interest of "Free Religion" — will sufficiently establish the correctness of these statements. The writers whom we quote are careful and acute thinkers, and, though differing on many points from each other, probably agree in the above statements.

Thus (in "The Radical," January, 1869) Mr. Samuel Johnson says that the declarations of Jesus concerning his own position show his exclusiveness and limitation. "Other teachers," he adds, "in that age, and prophets, stirred by a pure spontaneity in earlier ages, had trusted eternal truth to its own authority. And it is for ever true that the noblest form of spiritual affirmation is not that in which the teacher puts himself in the foreground, but that in which he hides behind the divinity of his message." The earlier teachers were, therefore, in this respect superior to Jesus. Final unity, he argues, must come from passing from Christ and Christianity into a larger theism.

In "The Radical" for August, 1868, Mr. O. B. Frothingham, in an article on the "Historical Position of Jesus," objects to Theodore Parker's well-known sonnet to Jesus. In this sonnet Mr. Parker says, —

> "Thy truth is still the light
> Which guides the nations groping on their way,
> Stumbling and falling in disastrous night,
> Yet hoping ever for the perfect day.
> Yes! thou art still the Life; thou art the Way
> The holiest know; Light, Life, and Way of heaven!
> And those who dearest hope and deepest pray
> Toil by the Light, Life, Way, which thou hast given."

Mr. Frothingham declares that it was sentiment, not science, which inspired this sonnet; and that it is a mere delusion or deceit to offer this Jesus of conjecture to mankind. Mr. Frothingham denies that Jesus was the founder of a church; or author either of a religion; of authority in belief, or ethics; or authority in faith. We know little or nothing about him; and, personally, he is nothing to us, — thinks Mr. Frothingham.

The editor of "The Radical" (April, 1868), in an article called "Humanity *versus* Christianity," says, "Humanity is universal. It is equality, unity, liberty, reason, progress, peace. Christianity is partial. It is aristocratic, limited in its development, slavish, at war with the free expansion of the human mind."

Mr. Abbot, in "The Index," — published at Toledo, in Ohio, — contrasts Christianity with Free Religion, and says (in his "Fifty Affirmations"):

"34. The completion of the religious protest against authority must be the extinction of Faith in the Christian Confession.

"35. Free Religion is emancipation from the outward law, and voluntary obedience to the inward law.

"50. Christianity is the faith of the soul's childhood; Free Religion is the faith of the soul's manhood. In the gradual growth of mankind out of Christianity into Free Religion, lies the only hope of the spiritual perfection of the individual and the spiritual unity of the race."

In our next chapter, we shall examine some of the criticisms of these writers on Christianity, and their objections to it. Our purpose now, in quoting them, is merely to show that they regard pure theism (or Free Religion) as an advance on Christianity: whereas we believe, and are prepared to show, that Christianity is an advance on theism.

But we must now ask, What is the distinction between them? Our answer is, — that Christianity is an historic religion, with a Founder, a church or communion, with its sacred books, its rites and ceremonies, its faith and its morality. These doctrines, worship, books, church, and morals, all have the historic person of Jesus for their centre and source.

Theism, or Free Religion, on the contrary, is a system of belief and method of life which grows up in the human mind, independently of any such historic source, proceeding only from the soul itself.

We are happy to be able to accept here one of Mr. Abbot's definitions. He says, — correctly as we think, —

"Christianity is the historic religion, taught in the Christian Scriptures, and illustrated in the history of the Christian Church."

Mr. Abbot gives us no definition of "Free Religion," except that he tells us that its ideal is self-development, and that its corner-stone is faith in human nature. But at all events, Free Religion rejects the authority of all historic religion, and goes back to the instincts of the individual as its origin and authority.

It has been usual for theologians to make other distinctions beside this. For example, they distinguish between natural and revealed religions, rationalism and supernaturalism, human and divine religions. We do not accept these definitions, nor regard them as strictly philosophical. All religions, which have any truth in them, are revealed, supernatural, and divine. If man ever truly sees God, it is by God's revealing himself. He reveals himself in the natural world, as well as in the spiritual world. God reveals his majesty and his benignity in the law of gravitation no less than in the life of Jesus. So, if "supernatural" means a violation of law, no religion is supernatural; if it means the manifestation of higher laws than those which commonly appear, then every religion has its supernatural side. In the same way, all religions are natural, rational, and human, so far as they contain truths and influences adapted to the needs of man. Christianity is a religion of nature, inasmuch as it meets the wants of human nature, tends to unfold human nature, and is in accord with human reason. A truly divine religion must also be truly human, rational, and natural. For this reason we set aside the old definitions, and distinguish Christianity from "theism" or "Free Religion," only as this definite, positive, and historic religion is distinguished from the religion of the individual reason, whose ideal is self-development, and which identifies true. freedom with a protest against all authority. Christianity is a particular historic religion: Free Religion is the effort of the solitary soul, seeking for truth, goodness, and beauty, by its own independent efforts.

We will now attempt to show why Christian theism is an advance on any kind of theism outside of Christianity.

Christianity, by its methods, goes down deeper, goes up higher, goes out more widely, and goes on further, than any other form of theism. It goes down deeper, because its essence is life, not thought, and life is deeper than thought. It goes up higher, because it obeys the law of mediation, by which alone ascent to the highest regions of divine truth and love becomes possible. It goes out more widely, because its central life, proceeding from Jesus, includes the germs of all human tendencies and human effort, and so is able to satisfy all wants. It goes on further, because its method of progress is that of evolution; preserving its spiritual identity, but advancing from form to form, according to the needs of every age.

We have not, of course, space in which to do more than indicate this argument. But we shall try to make the substance of it plain.

1. Christianity goes *deeper* than any other religion by its law of life.

It is easy to perceive that theism, wherever it has appeared outside of Christianity, has been essentially thought, while inside of Christianity it is essentially life. Theism reasons about God: Christianity lives from him and to him. Theism gives us speculations and probabilities; Christianity, convictions and realities. Not that theism undervalues spiritual and moral life, but that it seeks them by the path of thought, not that of spiritual communion. Nor does Christianity undervalue knowledge, but it seeks knowledge through life. Theism says light is the life of men; Christianity declares that life is the light of men. Now life can produce light; but light can seldom produce life. A living religion, even if it be narrow and shallow as that of Mohammed, is sure to create a great intellectual activity, though perhaps only a transient illumination, as was that of the Arabian scholars in the eighth century. Christianity—a life of faith, hope, and love—has in all ages stimulated to thought, created great scholars and writers, founded schools and colleges, and diffused knowledge among the people. A stream of spiritual and moral life always creates philosophy; but when did speculation or philosophy create a stream of life?

If philosophy could ever create life, it would have come from the Neo-Platonism of Alexandria in the second and third centuries after Christ. Some of the greatest thinkers and purest men the world has known then attempted to found a large unitary religion on the basis of an integral philosophy. Combining the vast ideas of oriental thought with the Greek philosophy, men like Plotinus, Porphyry, Iamblichus, Proclus, Synesius, aimed at the same result which is now attempted by the writers in the "Radical" and the "Index." They meant to replace Christianity by a grand system of thought, which should contain also the elements of religious life. But they made the mistake of trying to get life out of thought, instead of thought out of life; and so they failed.

Christianity is essentially a stream of spiritual, moral, and intellectual life, proceeding from Jesus of Nazareth. He did not present it as an intellectual system, but it overflowed from his lips in his daily intercourse with men. He did not speak from his speculation, but from his knowledge. He spoke what he knew, and testified what he had seen. This living knowledge created like convictions in other minds. The truth was its own evidence.

Man needs this knowledge. We need to know God, not merely to think it probable that he exists. We need to live in the light of his truth and his love. We do not get this knowledge of God by reading books of theology, but by communion with those who have it. If we have any such faith in God, how did we first obtain it? We caught it, as a blessed contagion, from the eyes and lips, the words freighted with conviction, the actions inspired by its force, of those who have been themselves filled with its power. They too usually received it first from others; though afterwards it may have been fed by direct communion with God. It is a transmitted, as well as an inspired life. It came from souls in whom God dwelt abundantly, and the fire of whose conviction kindled a flame in other hearts. This flame is continually fed anew by the great prophets of the race, whom God raises up, and fills with a double portion of his Spirit. And the deeper, purer, loftier they are, the more do they love to trace back the great master-impulse to

Jesus of Nazareth. "Of his fulness have we all received," say they, "and grace upon grace." As we see, in some families, the influence of a noble ancestor prolonged through many generations, so we see the life of Christ prolonged from century to century. To him God, the Father and Friend of all, was a reality and the greatest reality; the law of right as clear as the laws of the material universe; immortality as certain as the present life; and to him every man seemed truly a brother. Nothing but a faith like this, making inward realities as perfectly certain as outward realities, can explain the effect of Christ on the world. He lifted the human race to a higher plane where they could see God, duty, and immortal life, face to face. As the Nile flows thousands of miles through Africa, carrying fertility on its ample bosom,—issuing from the great basin and lakes around the Equator,—so, from this source has flowed a stream of moral life down to our day. Abandon this current of Christian civilization, and presently you find yourselves in a wilderness, a barren desert of mere speculation. God then becomes an opinion; duty, a social convenience; immortality, a perhaps.

We are so made that, while our opinions are sharpened and systematized by independent thought, our convictions are fed by the contact of living souls. This is the meaning of the Christian church. It is not an organization, a form, a creed; but wherever two or three really meet in the spirit of Jesus, there he is present in the midst of them. Living souls create, extend, re-create life in each other. When we reflect, reason, speculate, we go alone ; but when we need a new power of faith and conviction, then we go to others. We seek the humblest soul in which God dwells : we gather new strength from communion with all believing hearts. We put ourselves into the great current of a common faith ; and drink out of it new power, peace, and insight. We go to the people of God wherever they are ; and in their communion we are fed. Now this need of the soul leads us back to Jesus, as to that Vine in whom we are all branches. This fact illustrates what has been called the solidarity of the human race. The formula stated philosophically is this, "Man thinks alone ; but he lives in communion with others." And in our Christian religion, this common life is the life coming from Jesus of Nazareth. He says "Abide in me, and I in you. As the branch cannot bear fruit of itself except it abide in the vine, no more can ye except ye abide in me. I am the vine : ye are the branches."

But this law of communion is not recognized by the apostles of free religion. They take more pleasure in standing apart, to think ; than in coming together, to live. They even prefer speculation to knowledge. The highest of all virtues, with them, is the love of truth. And they would not be far wrong, were it not that they mistake, for the love of truth, the love of seeking after truth. And the love for seeking truth, rather than for finding it, naturally leads to another mistake. It makes them overvalue new opinions, and undervalue old ones. The old truths, already attained, do not give any opportunity to these strenuous seekers; therefore they desire novelty, and call men "brave thinkers" in the exact proportion in which they disagree with the rest of the world. Mr. Johnson (in his article on "The Fallacy of Supernaturalism") quotes with admiration the famous sentence of Lessing:

> "Not the truth which one possesses, or believes himself to possess, but the honest striving after truth, is what makes the worth of man. If God should hold all truth enclosed in his right hand, and in his left only the ever-active impulse to the pursuit of truth, although with the condition that I should for ever err; and should say to me Choose! I should fall with submission on his left hand, and say, Father, give! Pure truth is for thee alone."

But, with all respect for Lessing, is it not apparent that such a choice could not proceed from the love of truth? Apply it to scientific truth. What should we think of a chemist, a geologist, an astronomer, who should prefer to be always in scientific error, — provided he went wrong in seeking truth himself, — rather than to possess the truths of science, if he had to accept them as discovered and taught by others! We should not, I think, call him a strong lover of truth.

If thought could ever become a fountain of life, it would have done so in the case of Socrates. No more sincere, pure, generous seeker for truth has ever appeared on earth. He was, as Mr. Emerson says of himself, "an endless seeker, with no past behind him." But, though always seeking, he seldom found. The net result of his speculation, as he himself declares, was only the knowledge of his ignorance. He opens questions, but leaves them unsettled. He is a thinker, but not a teacher. He is a perfect illustration of the case supposed by Lessing, — of one to whom God opened the left hand of seeking truth, but not the right hand of truth itself. And what was the result of the generous labors of this great soul? The histories of Philosophy inform us that he founded no school, nor continuous movement of thought; but that his moral enthusiasm ended in the dogmatism of the Cynics, and the happiness doctrine of Aristippus; while his keen analytic irony produced the scepticism of Megaris and Elis.

The problem which Christianity solves, is the union of individual life and common life. The solitary, seeking God and truth, alone in his lonely hermitage, loses his love, grows cold, hard, and selfish. The philanthropist — always in the hurry of multifarious duties, never going apart to think and pray alone — becomes at last superficial, shallow, empty. Christianity feeds the individual soul by prayer, and communion with God; and enlarges the heart, by communion with Christian brethren and those human sufferers for whom Christ died. As in a tree there are ten thousand buds, and each bud has, not merely its own separate movement, but also partakes of the common life of the whole tree, — so it is in Christianity. Love to God purifies the soul and elevates its separate power: love to man warms it with human sympathy, and the joyful sense of a common human nature.

Christianity establishes a communion, and it is through such a communion that we receive moral life. The law of this life, proceeding from Jesus, consists in the alternation of interior solitary aspiration, with outward receptivity and activity in social intercourse. It thus becomes a communion with God, with Christ, and with the church. All prayer, worship, service, implies this reciprocal activity. Each soul has a life in itself, and a common life with others, which, by mutual action and reaction, are more and more unfolded. In Christianity, more than in any other religion, is the balance kept between the activity of the private and that of the church. In Romanism, the centripetal force, or church-life, predominates; in Protestantism, the centrifugal force, or the life of the individual, predominates: but in all parts of the church, and in all its epochs, both are found, mutually regulating and renewing each other's power.

2. Christianity goes higher than any other form of theism, by means of its law of mediation.

"There is one God," says the apostle, "and one Mediator between God and man, — the man Christ

Jesus." Free Religion rejects, with indignation, the idea of mediation. It declares itself unwilling to go to God through any other soul. It declares that every one ought to go directly to God. But Christianity, by its law of mediation, takes a higher flight than theism without it. By one man, in whom is the fulness of the divine and human, it brings God to all the races, classes, conditions, and characters of mankind. The doctrine of incarnation means that a perfect man becomes again, what Adam is reported to have been, the image of God. So, those who see him, see his Father. We look upon Christ, and in his life, words, sorrows, death, resurrection, we see expressed, in living symbols, the thoughts of the Almighty to his children. Thus God, — who is afar off when seen in nature, who is dimly manifested in the mysterious depths of the soul, — when seen through this human medium, comes near to his children as Father and Friend.

According to theism, every one must rise by personal struggle and solitary effort. But according to Christianity man rises by joining with this effort the readiness to receive and transmit the divine impulse of which Christ is the Mediator. Man does not make any less effort on this account, but more. By helping others, he helps himself. By becoming a mediator of this Christian life to other souls, he receives more in his own. The law is, "Give, and it shall be given you."

The universe of spiritual existence, we must needs believe, consists of a vast ascending order of moral, intellectual, and spiritual power. It is a hierarchy, in which are angels and archangels, thrones and dominions, rising above each other in a never-ending flight toward God. If the law of progress was merely that of self-culture, each one struggling to rise alone, higher and higher, the result would be a selfish isolation. But join to this the law of mediation, announced and illustrated by Jesus, and then one great life will flow down from God, along the whole series, to the lowest moral being that exists.

All variety tends to separation. Therefore the very effort of man to perfect himself (which Mr. Abbot declares to be religion) would, the more it was successful, only alienate man the more from man. Diversities of gifts, of education, of knowledge, of fidelity, enable some men to succeed far better than others in the effort to perfect themselves. One man has five talents, and gains other five talents, and becomes ruler over five cities. Another has only one, and loses even that, by not improving it. If this law of retribution were all of religion; if this natural law of consequences were the whole, — then, the more there was of religion, the more there would be of divergence. But this is compensated by the antagonist Christian law of mediation, by which he who exalteth himself is abased, and he who humbles himself is exalted. All true elevation consists, not in getting power, goodness, knowledge for ourselves, but that we may mediate these to others. Christ became perfect, not by trying to perfect himself, but by trying to help others. Because he came to seek and save the lost, because he humbled himself to the death of a slave on the cross, God has highly exalted him. His greatness and glory consist in mediating the infinite truth and love of God to his disciples, who, in turn, mediate it to others. Thus, the unity of the race, — lost irretrievably if Mr. Abbot's religion of "effort to perfect one's self" were all, — being supplemented by the effort to save others, is more than regained. The divine love, incarnate in Jesus, passes through him to his disciples, and to all mankind.

The life of which Jesus is the Mediator, and which flows through the communion of all who receive it, is the life of God, incarnate in man. The love and pity of Jesus, the truth and holiness of Jesus, are all emanations from heaven, descending into our world, to unite man with God, and man with man. But the divine love and truth come according to an order. Some receive them first, others later. It was ordained, in the providence of God, that Jesus should be the Mediator of the New Covenant. The Old Covenant is the religion of effort, which says, "Struggle to perfect yourself, and you shall reap as you sow." The New Covenant says to all, whether they are far or near, good or bad, perfect or imperfect, saints or sinners, "Receive God's love, flowing down from him, through Christ, and so become one with God, and one with each other."

The substance of Christianity, we have seen, is not thought, but life. But the essence of that life is the sight of God's truth and love, revealed through the mediation of Christ and his disciples, to save the souls of all mankind from sin and death. Therefore the doctrines of the incarnation and the atonement have always been the pivots of Christian theology. The incarnation means, God descending into the soul of one man to make all humanity divine, to unite earth with heaven, time with eternity, man with God. The elevation of the human race, so justly dear to the modern theist, is made possible by this great providential event in human history. By the law of mediated life, God is lifting humanity to himself, and penetrating the boundless variety of his creation with as pervasive a unity. When Jesus said, "I and my Father are one;" "he that hath seen me, hath seen the Father;" and then went on to declare that the glory God had given to him, he had given to his disciples, that they might be one, as he and his Father were one, "I in them, and thou in me, that they may be made perfectly one,"— he taught those great vital truths which theologians have poorly expressed by the doctrines of incarnation, mediation, and atonement.

The doctrines have never yet been satisfactorily defined. But the facts, underlying these doctrines, have always constituted the power of Christianity. The Christian life of love to God and love to man is evermore renewed in the soul, by receiving God's redeeming love, mediated through Christ, and uniting us with God and man. There is no other force so vital, so inexhaustible, as this. It penetrates to the lowest depths in every heart; it reaches the deepest experience of evil; it transmutes sin into penitent and grateful love. There is no soul so high as to have outsoared this influence, none too low to be found by it.

By means of this law of mediation, Christianity makes a great advance on every form of theism which omits it. Theism, without this truth, can only tell men to perfect themselves by their own efforts. This may be enough for the strong and courageous. But it does not meet the wants of the discouraged, the weak, the sinful. These need more than the sight of law: they need that experience of forgiving love, of which Christ is the Mediator in this world. When we say that Christ is the Mediator of God's forgiving love to the sinner, we merely assert a fact: we do not state a theory. That he is such a Mediator is no matter of theory; for the whole experience of the Christian church declares that Jesus has brought this priceless boon to the human soul. Those who were afar off are made nigh by the blood of Jesus. His death and resurrection have set the seal on this great atoning power, which is as effective now to create love to God and to man as it was in the beginning.

We must distinguish between the facts of the incarnation and atonement, and the theories concerning them. The church doctrines of trinity, incarnation, and atonement, may be all wrong. The history of doctrines seems to show that they have never as yet received an adequate statement; since very opposite views on these points have been regarded as orthodox at different periods. But, though we may freely criticise the theology, let us beware lest we lose sight of the facts behind and below the theology. The theology has been only an imperfect language, by which the human mind has feebly attempted to state its experiences. An imperfect language is better than none. The popular heart has been willing to make use of any theology which seemed to express its conviction, that, somehow, God comes near to the soul in Jesus Christ; that, somehow, through Jesus Christ our sense of sin is taken away; that, through Christ, mortal fears are replaced by an immortal hope. Enough. Call it trinity, call it atonement, call it incarnation, call it an expiatory sacrifice, call it a mediatorial work, — the fact remains unaltered in all Christian experience, that, when we look at the life, the death, the work, the spirit of Jesus, we are brought into the peace of God. What is the chaff to the wheat?

Higher than this communion with God, no religion can go. Other religions sometimes attain to it, but usually by the special efforts of select souls. In Christianity God comes to all, and comes always. "My Father and I will come and make our abode with him."

3. Christianity goes out more widely in its sympathy with man than any other religion.

By this we intend the universality of Christianity. Theism accuses it of being narrow. Free Religion declares that Christianity is limited by a creed, which consists in professing faith in Jesus as the Christ. No doubt if this be a creed, Christianity adheres to it, in all sects and all denominations. To adhere to Jesus as the Christ of God, is the very root of Christian experience.

But does this make Christianity narrow? We think there is no religion in the world which has such elements of catholicity, because there is no religion which is inspired by so deep a life. All that is in Brahminism of truth, and all that is in Buddhism; all the good that Socrates sought, Confucius declared, and Zoroaster saw, — all these are to be found, as essential and vital elements of Christian life. Other religions are the religions of races: Christianity, from the very beginning, overleaped the barriers of nationality and of race, and found its disciples in all lands and classes.

Christianity is, by its principles, as broad as human nature. It knows no distinction of Brahmin and Sudra, of initiated and uninitiated. It comes to all, high and low, rich and poor, bond and free, male and female. There is no other religion so catholic: its aim is to be the religion of the human race. Therefore it has always been a missionary religion, seeking to make converts in heathen lands. Before the Goths conquered the Roman Empire, Christianity had conquered them. It has never found a race which could not be

Christianized. The half-frozen Esquimaux in Greenland were converted by the Moravians, and the life of Christ melted their rude hearts into gratitude. The fierce Frank, hearing the story of the death of Jesus, cried out in a passion of horror, "Why was not I there with my brave Franks, to prevent it?" The Saxon thanes came together in a great building, open on all sides, to hear the Christian missionary tell his story. They listened with attention, and, when he had finished, one of them rose and said, "Brother thanes, this man has come from far, to tell us of God and the future. If he has any thing to tell us, let us hear him. For to me it seems that our life is like the flight of that little bird, which just flew into this hall, out of the dark night, — flashed through, lighted for a moment by the blaze of our fire, and then out again into darkness on the other side. We came out of darkness: we go into darkness. If he can tell us any thing, let us hear it."

When Father Marquette discovered the Upper Mississippi, he met tribes of Indians, at war with each other, and each received him kindly, but told him that the next tribe on the river would kill him. But he went on, armed only with Christian faith and love; and still found his way to their rude hearts, as he followed the windings of the beautiful stream.

From the little child, who has just learned to say "Our Father in heaven," to the great intellect of a Shakspeare and a Milton; from the pure saint, giving all of life to charity and prayer, to the lost child of sin, freezing in the streets of some roaring Babylon; from the culture of Paris to the barbarism of Australia,— Christianity goes and comes, and has a word of truth and love for all. None are above the gospel, none below it. It reaches down its beneficent hands to lift the leper whom no one else will touch; to instruct the Samaritan, outside of all healthy religious organizations; to comfort the publican and sinner; to enlighten the groping unbeliever. It has depths where the elephant must swim, shallows where the child can wade. It has mysteries which the angels desire to look into, and simplicities which he who runs may read. Herein consists the breadth of Christianity. It has the power to reach all sorts of people, because it has something for all. It offers forgiveness to the sinner, peace to the troubled, comfort to the sorrowful, immortal hope to the bereaved. It teaches the rich how to use their riches, and the poor how to be contented without them. To the ignorant it brings light, in its schools, its books, its teachers: to the learned, it gives the key to deeper knowledge, and the means of using their learning for good ends. By its variety of sects, creeds, and ceremonies, it meets the various tastes and tendencies of the soul. To those who love form, it offers a gorgeous ritual; to those who seek simplicity, it opens a Quaker Meeting or a Methodist Conference; to thinkers, it gives infinite subject for speculation; to practical persons it offers works of charity and benevolence. For those who love beauty and art, it has its architecture; its majestic cathedrals; its sublime music; its immortal paintings of prophet and sibyl, holy martyr and tender Madonna. Thus it shows its breadth by harmonizing all antagonisms in its large communion, its ample reconciliation; bringing so many varieties into unity; making the cow and the bear feed together, and the lion lie down with the lamb.

This is the work it is doing in the world. It has not done it as yet: if it had, the millennium had arrived. But while, outside of Christendom, piety wars with humanity, faith with works, ascetic religion with earthly joy, order with freedom, law with liberty; and so we have despotism with order here, anarchy with liberty there; religion and gloom on one side, joy and licentiousness on the other: within Christianity we find a principle at work which makes it possible to be free yet obedient; humble, but hopeful; self-denying, but cheerful; pure, yet gay; holding the love of God without asceticism, and the love of man without atheism. It is broad as the nature of man, and so meets it everywhere.

This is the breadth of Christianity. It is like that of the ocean, everywhere embracing the land; thundering against the glaciers of Greenland, kissing the sands of Florida; adapting itself to every form of every coast; and rolling its tidal wave into every gulf, sea, and estuary in all the zones, and around every continent.

No doubt Christianity has often been forced into a creed, — a Roman-Catholic creed, or a Calvinistic creed, — according to the small theory of some small party or sect. But Christianity itself, unconscious of these little limits, continually passes beyond them, and outgrows them, leaving them all behind. So have we seen little boys trying to dam up a running brook with stones and sticks; but the brook undermines their dike, and runs under it, — rises and overflows it, and sweeps it away. No creed made by man has ever been able to restrain the expansive force of the gospel. Its stream of life is like one of our New-England rivers, barricaded by dikes and dams all the way. Christianity has been compelled to turn the wheels of innumerable sects, each manufacturing in its mill some patent religion of its own. The patient river turns them all, but moves on, and leaves them all behind. All may use it; but not one can monopolize it. Christianity is not a mill, grinding out special opinions, — but an influence, creating innumerable forms of thought, but not itself bound by any. Sometimes, in its affluence, it rises in a freshet of thought, as in the Protestant Reformation, and sweeps the dams and mills away. Christianity is not a creed, but a life, proceeding from Jesus Christ.

4. Christianity is an advance on theism, because it has a greater power of progress than any other religion.

There are two methods of human progress, which

may be designated as progress by revolution and progress by evolution. The first is illustrated by the movement of a body through space, the other by the growth of a plant or of an animal. The comet, moving toward the sun, must quit one point entirely in order to reach another: the tree, evolved from a seed, takes its past with it as it goes. The human soul may make progress by change or by growth. It will, in the first case, move forward from a low position to a higher one, leaving its past behind it for ever. To-day forgets yesterday: to-morrow will forget to-day. Or it may, without any quarrel with its previous life, and holding all it has gained, continue to gain more. Both methods of progress are good; but the last is the best.

The intellect makes progress either by contending against error, seeing mistakes and leaving them, being converted from one view to the opposite; or else, by calmly growing up from truth into larger truth, from the insight of to-day into the deeper insight of to-morrow; enlarging past knowledge, not leaving it. Society makes progress either by revolutions or by reforms. The surest progress is always of the latter sort: the best reform is not that which destroys and annuls the past, but that which fulfils it. Science, to-day, has commonly accepted the idea of change by development, for that of change by crisis.

Now, in the place of the Christian law of progress by evolution, the teachers of free religion seem inclined to substitute an attempt at progress by revolution. Instead of developing Christianity into some higher Christianity, they desire to step outside of it altogether, and begin a new movement on the *tabula rasa* of simple human nature. They propose to drop Jesus Christ, as something outgrown; to ignore all historic Christianity as insignificant; to eliminate the marvellous element from the life of Jesus, as being no better than old wives' fables, — and so to start fair with the postulates of pure unembarrassed reason. But is this really progress; or is it relapse?

It is true that Mr. Abbot, and other writers of his school, speak of Free Religion as a growth from Christianity; and no doubt they may regard it as a natural development. But in progress by evolution the identity is preserved throughout. The Christianity of Jesus, reaching backward, identified itself with the oldest patriarchal religion, and declared that before Abraham was, he was the Christ. It found itself in the prophetic predictions, and saw that it grew naturally out of them. Therefore, both Catholics and Protestants keep the patriarchal, levitical, and prophetic religious books as an essential part of their own Sacred Scriptures. But Free Religion does not identify itself with Christianity, nor with Judaism. It steps out from the Christian church, sets aside the Christian tradition, disclaims allegiance to the Christian Head, and becomes "an endless seeker, with no past behind it."

Every Christian sect, even the most heretical, holds to the root, clings to Jesus, and considers itself as the ripe, consummate flower of that tree. Free Religion differs from all Christian sects in this, — that it does not profess to be *true* Christianity, according to the mind of Jesus, but to be something better than Jesus ever saw or intended. Its root is not in Christianity, but in science and civilization. Its Bibles are the last works on chemistry, geology, astronomy. Its prophets are Huxley, Spencer, Mill, Tyndall, and Comte. It sits at their feet, and hears their words, with an almost implicit faith. It abhors every priesthood, save the critical and scientific sacerdotalism. To that, it bows down in mute and reverential awe. Though it may honestly believe itself to be the natural outcome of Christianity, it must be evident to itself, when it considers the matter, that it has lost its connection with that root. It no longer abides in Christ, nor does it desire to do so.

No doubt some existing religions are older than Christianity. That of Confucius is older by five centuries. The Jews, in their synagogues, can go back for their Passover to a law delivered to them at least thirteen centuries before the birth of Jesus. The sacred books of the Brahmins are perhaps older still. But the question is not of duration, but of progress. These three have long since ceased to make any progress. They live by their past. But Christianity is as young as ever. It is in a constant process of development. It came out of Judaism; it then developed out of Jewish Christianity into the universalism of Paul; and, lastly, out of Romanism into Protestantism. In the early centuries came from its roots such shoots as the great monastic orders, who did so much to civilize Europe. From it, in later days, have come Puritanism, Quakerism, Wesleyism, Unitarianism, Universalism, Swedenborgianism. Foolish people are afraid of these divisions, and think them a sign of decay. But in truth they are tokens of perennial growth. As the age advances, Christianity comes to meet it, in some new form, putting the new wine into new bottles.

Jesus foretold that a Christianity should come different from any he had been able to teach. He said that the Spirit of truth should take of his truth, and teach many things at some future time to those who were not able to bear them then. The Divine Spirit of truth has, during eighteen centuries, been teaching to the church a deeper and a nobler Christianity than it before knew. A great deal of Judaism and of Paganism adhered to the early church. Much of it has been outgrown: some of it remains. But the Christian church has, in its moral nature, a *vis medicatrix*, by which it can cure its own diseases. It has a power of growth, by which it can lift itself above itself, and evolve a higher life from year to year. There is no evidence that this process is approaching its end. Christianity is as fresh and young as on the day of its creation. It is not likely to be superseded, or to be passed by.

Thus, in all the dimensions of space, we find in Christianity something in advance of theism. It is deeper in its life, higher in its aspiration, broader in its sweep, more far-reaching in its perpetual advance.

In one magnificent sentence, the apostle Paul has summed up all our argument. He tells the Ephesians that his prayer for them is, "That Christ may dwell in your hearts by faith; that ye, being rooted and grounded in love, may be able to comprehend with all saints what is the breadth, and length, and depth, and height; and to know the love of Christ, which passeth knowledge, that ye might be filled with all the fulness of God." In this language, borrowed from the dimensions of space, he already announces the imcomprehensible depth, exhaustless vitality, unlimited power of development and expansion, and vast inclusiveness of the Christian principle of love to Christ. Love to Christ is the method of progress, the law of freedom, the way to knowledge, and the unchecked impulse to God.

At present, we do not see that Free Religion can offer us any motive, insight, purity, or humanity, which Christianity does not contain in a much fuller degree. All its best ideas and noblest spirit it has received from this great mother. The parts of Christianity which lie outside of its experience, it rejects as weak and false: the parts which suit it, it reproduces as its own. Some simple Christians, who have all their lives been taught these same truths out of the Bible, receive them as novelties when offered under the name of Free Religion. They are like the philosopher in Lowell's poem, who gratefully received as a present the fruit stolen from his own garden.

> "When they send him a dishful, and ask him to try 'em,
> He never suspects how the sly rogues came by 'em;
> He wonders why 'tis there are none such his trees on,
> And thinks them the best he has tasted this season."

But we see no reason for fearing that Christianity is to be outgrown or passed by. It comes out of the fore-ordination of God in the earliest past: it reaches forward into the remotest future. It sweeps together, in its large embrace, all races, characters, intellects, conditions. Beings in heaven, and on earth, and under the earth, bow before the great name of Christ, and confess him to be Lord, to the glory of God the Father. It sinks into the deepest depth of human experience, and gives the practical solution of the problems of human destiny. It rises on the wings of humility, fidelity, and love, to the highest heaven, to the living throne of God, around which collect

> "The spirits and intelligences fair,
> And angels waiting by the Almighty's chair."

Such are the simplicities and infinities of the gospel; simple as infancy, infinite as the universe of God.

CHAPTER IV.

Some Objections to Christianity Considered.

IN all the centuries, since Christianity commenced its great career, it has advanced in the face of opposition, and this opposition has often come from the highest intelligence of the age. No recent attacks on the Gospels can be compared, in respect to their power of insight, subtlety of logic, and weight of reason, with those which proceeded from philosophers like Celsus in the second century, or Porphyry in the third. At one time, during the eighteenth century, the best intelligence of the world seemed banded to the overthrow of the Christian religion. Tindal and Bolingbroke in England; Voltaire, Helvetius, and Diderot, in France; Lessing and Basedow, in Germany, — all contributed to a work which many feared was to extinguish Christianity for ever. Such assaults have, however, invariably resulted in a new development of Christian life and thought. The present attempt of many intelligent persons to furnish an improvement on Christianity, under the name of "Free Religion," will, no doubt, share the fate of previous movements in that direction. Christianity is not a theory which may be destroyed by criticism or new investigations. It is a stream of life pouring forth continually from its deep fountain, and flowing on through heat and cold, sometimes in a fuller or shallower current, but flowing on always, "Volvitur et volvetur, in omne volubilis ævum."

One objection to Christianity is, that Jesus accepted the office of the Jewish Christ, or Messiah.

This criticism, urged against Jesus by many of the Radical writers, is thus condensed by Mr. Abbot in his "Fifty Affirmations:"

RELATION OF JUDAISM TO CHRISTIANITY.

10. The idea of a coming "kingdom of heaven" arose naturally in the Hebrew mind after the decay of the Davidic monarchy, and ripened under foreign oppression into a passionate longing and expectation.

11. The "kingdom of heaven" was to be a world-wide empire on this earth, both temporal and spiritual, to be established on the ruins of the great empires of antiquity by the miraculous intervention of Jehovah.

12. The Messiah or Christ was to reign over the "kingdom of heaven" as the visible deputy of Jehovah, who was considered the true sovereign of the Hebrew nation. He was to be a Priest-King, — the supreme pontiff or high-priest of the Hebrew church, and absolute monarch of the Hebrew state.

13. The "apocalyptic literature" of the Jews exhibits the gradual formation and growth of the idea of the Messianic "kingdom of heaven."

14. All the leading features of the gospel doctrine concerning the "kingdom of heaven," the "end of the world," the "great day of judgment," the "coming of the Christ in

the clouds of heaven," the "resurrection of the dead," the "condemnation of the wicked and the exaltation of the righteous," the "passing away of the heavens and the earth," and the appearance of a "new heaven and a new earth," were definitely formed and firmly fixed in the Hebrew mind, in the century before Jesus was born.

15. John the Baptist came preaching that "the kingdom of heaven is at hand." But he declared himself merely the forerunner of the Messiah.

16. Jesus also came preaching that "the kingdom of heaven is at hand," and announced himself as Messiah or Christ.

17. Jesus emphasized the spiritual aspect of the Messianic kingdom; but, although he expected his throne to be established by the miraculous intervention of God, and therefore refused to employ human means in establishing it, he nevertheless expected to discharge the political functions of his office as King and Judge, when the fulness of time should arrive.

18. As a preacher of purely spiritual truth, Jesus probably stands at the head of all the great religious teachers of the past.

19. As claimant of the Messianic crown, and founder of Christianity as a distinct historical religion, Jesus shared the spirit of an unenlightened age, and stands on the same level with Gautama or Mohammed.

20. In the belief of his disciples, the death, resurrection, and ascension of Jesus would not prevent the establishment of the "kingdom of heaven." His throne was conceived to be already established in the heavens; and the early church impatiently awaited its establishment on earth at the "second coming of the Christ."

21. Christianity thus appears as simply the complete development of Judaism, — the highest possible fulfilment of the Messianic dreams based on the Hebrew conception of a "chosen people."

The charge made against Jesus, in these paragraphs, is, that he made a Jewish view of the Messiah his own, and so accepted an error. But suppose the Jewish idea of the Messiah was, in its essence true, — would it be error then in Jesus to accept it?

Mr. Abbot and his sympathizers assume, without proving it, in a very unscientific way for the founders of a "scientific theology," that whatever the Jews believed must be erroneous. But is not the Jew a man? Is not Judaism, according to their view, a development of human nature? Has not a Jew eyes, hands, organs, dimensions, like other men? If you prick him, will he not bleed? How then does it necessarily follow that because a Jew believed in the "kingdom of heaven" as something to come upon earth, it must therefore be an error, and Jesus also in error in accepting it?

In the "10th affirmation" (as quoted above), Mr. Abbot tells us that the idea of the "'kingdom of heaven' arose naturally in the Hebrew mind after the decay of the Davidic monarchy." But Mr. Abbot's conception of true religion is, that it "arises naturally" in the human soul, and is not sent supernaturally. If, then, this idea of the kingdom of heaven "arose naturally," why is it to be assumed to be false, before investigation?

Every great and commanding idea, essentially true, is apt to gather around it secondary notions of an erroneous and mythical character. All births of time are subject to this law. But the real questions to ask in this case are, "What is the essential meaning in the Messianic idea?" and, "Is this essential meaning true or false?"

The "kingdom of heaven" means, simply, the reign of God on earth. Is this expectation false? On the contrary, is not the whole hope of humanity contained in the view that a time is to come in which God's will shall be done on earth, perfectly and entirely? The triumph of right over wrong, of good over evil, of truth over error, — this is the undying human hope. And this also is the substance of the Messianic idea.

The original conception of the Messiah and of his time, as it is found in the prophets, is, that an age shall arrive when God's laws shall be universally obeyed. The Messiah is to be both temporal and spiritual Ruler of this kingdom under God, — temporal, because his kingdom is to be a visible community, existing in time, and localized on earth; spiritual, because it is to be governed, not by force, but by truth and goodness. He is to be Priest and King (as Mr. Abbot correctly says): Priest, by his inward religious influence on the individual; King, by his outward civilizing influence on society. The chief marks of the Messiah's reign, according to the prophets, are these: —

1. The Messiah is to rule, not by force, but by the power of truth and goodness. This appears from such passages as these: "He shall smite the earth with the rod of his mouth, and with the breath of

his lips shall he slay the wicked." (Isaiah xi: 4.) "Righteousness shall be the girdle of his loins, and faithfulness the girdle of his reins." (Isaiah xi. 5.) The idea of force is secondary and subsequent.

2. In the new kingdom, instead of the outward law of Judaism, — the law of authority which governs external actions, — there is to be a law of love, making men do right not from the compulsion of conscience, but from simple joy in doing right. This is expressed in the passage in Jeremiah (xxxi. 31), "Behold the days come, saith the Lord, that I will make a new covenant with the house of Israel . . . will put my law in their inward parts, and write it in their hearts; and will be their God, and they shall be my people. And they shall teach no more every man his neighbor, and every man his brother, saying, Know the Lord: for they shall all know me, from the least of them unto the greatest of them, saith the Lord: for I will forgive their iniquity, and will remember their sin no more." This passage is quoted in the New Testament (Heb. viii. 8; x. 16), and applied to Christianity.

3. The dominion of the Messiah is not to be confined to the Jews, but is to extend over all other nations. Numerous passages express this idea; for example, the passage in Isaiah ii. 2–4, in which it is not only said that "all nations" shall flow into the house of Jehovah, but that the law shall "go forth from Zion," and that Jehovah shall become the Ruler

of the nations. In other places it is said that Jehovah shall "sprinkle many nations" (or purify them); that "the veil which is over all nations shall be destroyed;" that he shall "gather all nations and tongues to see his glory," &c.

4. In the days of this great kingdom of God, the woes, wrongs, and sins of the world are to cease. Notably, war is to cease, and a universal reconciliation take place. The wolf shall dwell with the lamb, the cow and the bear feed together. The earth shall be full of the knowledge of Jehovah. The desert shall blossom as a rose. There shall, in sum, be a new heavens and a new earth.

In the apocalyptic literature, these elements of the Messianic age—viz., a moral power, extending over all nations, substituting inward love for outward conformity, and so producing outwardly complete unity in all spheres—were carried much further. At the same time these noble ideas became mixed with lower conceptions. In the Sibylline writings, the book of Henoch, the fourth book of Esdras, the book of Jubilees, and the Targums, we find what a clear and strong conception of the Messiah and his kingdom took form in the Jewish mind as early as B. C. 160. God, say the Sibylline oracles, shall send a king from the sun, when the need of man is sorest, and wars are fiercest, and he shall cause wars to cease, and cause all men to recognize the immortal God. The book of Henoch calls the Messiah always "the Son of man,' and "the elect One," who shall open "a fountain of righteousness," and "fountains of wisdom," where all shall come and drink. Esdras describes the Messiah as a man rising from the mysterious sea, and flying in the clouds of heaven, and coming down and calling together "a peaceable multitude." At last, he says, "Christ shall die, and all that have breath," and "the earth return to its old silence." Then all souls shall come to judgment, truth shall stand, and faith bud, time end, and eternity begin.

In the midst of these ideas, Jesus was born and brought up. It was, no doubt, in regard to these opinions, that he talked to the wise men on that memorable occasion, when, absorbed in the longing for truth, he forgot father, mother, and home. He penetrated to the depth of this Messianic hope, until at last it became clear to him that if a man could be found, who should be both priest and king in the highest sense, he would be the Messiah of God. If he could manifest the true God so fully that men should see him as their father, and become his children,—that would be the Priesthood. If he could bear witness to the truth with such commanding authority that all well-disposed men, loving truth, should receive it and obey it, then he would be King. This work Jesus assumed and accomplished; he emancipated Judaism from its forms, and it became, in the hands of his apostles, a universal religion. That this was his intention appears from many passages, for example when the request of the Greeks to see him led him to the thought that if he died, he should draw all men unto him. He was to be King, as he tells Pilate, by bearing witness to the truth. In his sermon on the mount he fulfils the prophecy of changing the old covenant into a new one, by writing the law in the heart.

Mr. Abbot, and his associates, say that in claiming the Messianic crown Jesus "shared the spirit of an unenlightened age." Is it sharing the spirit of an unenlightened age, to take men where they are, and lead them on to the highest, deepest, and broadest truth. If Jesus had not only met the Jews on their own ground, but remained with them there, there would be some foundation for the charge. But it was because Jesus would not accept the low Jewish belief about the Messiah, but insisted on giving them that higher Jewish conception which was the step out of Judaism into a universal religion, that he died. He died a martyr to his spiritual conception of the work of the Messiah. His life was a ransom paid to free his nation from the slavery of the letter, and to restore them to the freedom of the spirit, the glorious liberty of the sons of God.

Mr. Abbot also informs us that Jesus "shared the spirit of an unenlightened age," by founding Christianity as a distinct historic religion. There may be a difference of opinion as to the best way of teaching religious truth. Some may believe the best way to sow seed to be to scatter it at random on the grass, rocks, road, by the wayside, among thorns, and where there is no depth of soil. Jesus thought otherwise. He considered that it was necessary to plant it in good, well-prepared ground, in order that it should bring forth thirty, fifty, and a hundred fold. He did not accept the "wayside" plan of sowing seed.* He planted his truth in the prepared soil of Judaism. Though unacquainted with modern science, he held to the law of evolution. He came not to destroy the law, but to fulfil it, by carrying it to its ultimate results, and causing it to be transfigured in a higher form. This, according to Mr. Abbot, was "an unenlightened method," nevertheless it resulted in making Christianity the religion of civilized man.

Mr. Abbot supposes that he has dealt a fatal blow at Christianity in calling it "simply the complete development of Judaism." But suppose that the theory should be finally accepted which regards man as simply the highest development of the monkey, would that make humanity any less human than it is now? If the universal religion is grown out of previous religions, is it any less universal because of that? If the "Messianic dreams" are fulfilled in the manifestation of a

* Some of his followers, however, seemed to think he did. There is a little hymn which exhorts us to "Fling, fling the wayside seed," as though the object of the parable were to recommend sowing at random.

King of truth and a Priest of love, is he any the less the world's King and the world's Priest on that account? If the Hebrew conception of "a chosen people" is at last found to signify that they are a people chosen to be the soil from which grows up the religion of human nature, shall the religion of human nature be considered as damaged by that fact?

It is also objected by our radical friends, that if we call Jesus "Lord and Master," this is a creed, and that it limits our freedom and checks our progress. All, however, depends on what we mean by "Master." There are two kinds of masters. The one kind enslaves us: the other sets us free. One master goes before the flock, and the sheep follow him where they wish to go to find pasture. Another goes behind the flock, and drives the sheep where they do not wish to go. The good master inspires us: the poor master merely orders us. The one acts upon us by reason and love; the other by will, force, and fear. One is a friend, the other a despot. The one makes us his disciples, the other his slaves. It is a good thing to have a master of the good kind; some one who shall feed our soul, inspire our mind, animate our life.

The mastership of Jesus is not that of constraint or compulsion. He never meant it to be so. His disciples have often made it so, — calling down fire from heaven to destroy those who, they believe, are opposed to their Master. But Jesus never sought to compel men to be his disciples. "All that the Father giveth me shall come to me," he says. He did not care to hear them say, "Lord! Lord!" He did not wish to arrest their faith and fix it on his own person: he wished it to go through him to God. He said, "He that believeth on me, believeth not on me, but on him that sent me; and he that seeth me, seeth him that sent me." He would not judge those who disbelieved him: he left it for the truth to judge them. "The good shepherd," he says, "goes before his sheep, and they follow him, for they know his voice." When his hearers could not understand him, he explained; when they objected, he gave a reason. All the long series of exquisite illustrations, which we call parables, were told to make his meaning clear when they could understand him; or to be like little boxes, to keep it in their memory till they were able to understand it. It seems to us, therefore, a proof of extreme narrowness and prejudice that some of the modern teachers of Free Religion should base on this fact, that Jesus taught in stories, the charge that he had a secret doctrine for his disciples differing from the public doctrine which he communicated to the people. It was because they had hardened their hearts so as not to be able to take in his plain teaching of the spiritual nature of the kingdom of the Messiah, as given in the sermon on the mount, that he adopted the plan of teaching by parables.*

* If Jesus taught an esoteric doctrine to his disciples which he did not teach to the common people, what was it? What was the distinction between the public and private doctrine

In whatever sense Jesus claimed to be Lord and Master, it was certainly not as demanding any blind assent to his teaching. It was not because he wished to hear the word "Lord" applied to him. It was not that he would accept any man the sooner as a real disciple, because he used the phrase "Master," or would reject him because he did not use it. One text is enough to prove this. "Not every one that saith unto me, Lord! Lord! shall enter into the kingdom of heaven; but he that doeth the will of my Father who is in heaven." He wishes our minds to be active, not passive, in listening to him.

There are Christian teachers, I know, who claim a different authority for Jesus than that reverence which accumulates around a teacher whose words have fed, with light and life, the intellect of nations and the heart of mankind. They wish that, instead of looking up to him with expectation, we should bow down before him with awe, and blindly accept his words. I

---

of Jesus? Has any one of the thousand critics of the Gospels pointed out such a distinction? If he distrusted the common people, it was curious that they heard him gladly. The only fact adduced in support of this statement is, that Jesus taught in parables; that is, in allegories and stories. But the meaning of these is sufficiently transparent to those who are not blinded by prejudice. So far from wishing to conceal his meaning in parables, Jesus was surprised to find that his disciples needed any explanation of them. What are the mysteries in the parables of the Prodigal Son, the Good Samaritan, the Talents?

shall show that this kind of authority he never asserted. He never asked for assent, but always sought to produce conviction.

It is true that Jesus continually declared that he was the door, the way, the truth, the life. He asked men to come to him, to believe in him, to become one with him. And this was not only his right, but his duty, on the supposition that he knew that he saw plainly God's everlasting truth. It was God's truth which he thus called them to see, in calling them to himself. It was because God's truth was incarnate in his life, that he said that he was the life. If this was a mistake; if his truth was not the absolute, eternal truth of God, — then he was wrong in this course. But if, on the other hand, he did not merely speculate and conjecture and reason, like Socrates, but saw and knew the truth, then it was his duty and his right to utter these great invitations.

There are three kinds of authority, — first, the authority of knowledge; second, of office; third, of character or personality. The authority of knowledge is that inexplicable power of utterance which belongs to one who really knows what he is speaking of. It gives clearness to his statements; makes them luminous, exhaustive, consistent; clothes them with the picturesque garb of life; and fills them with weight and substance. This was the authority which the people recognized in the sermon on the mount; for, at that time, Jesus was not known, and so had no personal authority; had not claimed to be the Messiah, and so had no official authority.

The authority of office, we all understand. This only belonged to Jesus after he was recognized as the Christ, and accepted as such, and only had weight with those who thus accepted him.

But personal authority is that influence which gradually accumulates around one, whose wisdom, goodness, character, have created reverence. It is one of the great educating influences in the world. When I go to Plato, Dante, Shakspeare, I go with expectation and faith. I feel sure that what they say, though I cannot at once understand it, has meaning and value. That which, coming from an unknown source, I should at once reject, coming from these mighty masters, I ponder and endeavor to penetrate. So, at last, I come to see what I never saw before; to feel my soul enlarged, deepened, and elevated. Thus personal authority exercises over us an educating influence.

But because we attribute either of these varieties of authority to a master, it does not follow that we are to receive his *dicta* blindly. A blind and passive reception of truth, is equivalent to not receiving it at all. The legitimate influence of authority is to inspire reverent, patient, expectant thought. It opens the mind to truth, and prepares it to receive it. The illegitimate influence of authority is to cause us to assent to the letter, to receive passively the form, to acquiesce in the conclusion, without really seeing or knowing the truth.

Now that Jesus always endeavored to produce conviction, and never cared for a mere external assent, appears from such facts as these: —

(*a*) His habit of arguing by means of analogies taken from common life and the laws of nature.

When he was asked why he mingled so familiarly with publicans and sinners, and objections were made to him on that account, on the principle *noscitur a sociis*, — he did not reply merely by saying, "I am the Son of God, and have official authority to do as I please." No; but he used the familiar analogy of the physician. "You might as well" — I suppose him to say — "find fault with a physician for going among sick people, and accuse him of having a very morbid taste, in so doing. Why does he always call on sick people, never on well people? *My* sick people are these sinners."

When the authority of John the Baptist and of the Pharisees was quoted against him, and it was intimated that it might be well for him to conform to the custom of fasting, and not run counter to public prejudice by omitting this religious observance, he again replied, not by saying, "I have as good a right as John the Baptist to say what my disciples shall do." Instead of this, he gave the rationale of fasting. It was an expression of grief, of a sense of emptiness and want. "My disciples do not experience this need while I am with them. You do not ask the guests at a marriage to fast, and complain of them that they look glad and not sad. That which is suitable at one time is not suitable at another."

In teaching the providence of God, he does not rest his argument on his own inspiration, but on the analogies of nature. "If God clothe the grass of the field, shall he not much more clothe you?"

In showing that God will always answer the prayer for spiritual blessings, he relies on the analogies of human life. "What man who is a father would not give bread to a hungry child?" He appeals to no personal or official authority, but to the pure instincts of human nature, in support of his teaching.

(*b*) His frequent practice of leading on the mind of his hearers by questions, until he made them see clearly what he wished them to believe.

Thus on the memorable occasion which resulted in the story of the good Samaritan, we are told that a teacher of the law came to test the knowledge of Jesus. He probably had a plan laid to make the Master contradict himself. The "lawyer" first asked the apparently innocent question, "What shall I do to inherit eternal life?" Perhaps he expected that Jesus would reply, "Believe in me and become my disciple." Then he would have gone on and asked, "Why should I believe in you? Are you the Messiah?" But whatever his plan may have been, Jesus turned his position by simply asking him what he himself, as one skilled in the law, would give as the answer to his own question. And when he replied, "Love God, and love my neighbor," "Yes," said the Master: "you know it; now do it." The man of theology, not well pleased that his difficulty turned out to be no difficulty at all, made a new puzzle about the extent of meaning involved in "neighbor." Then Jesus tells the parable, which has been the instruction of all time. At its close the lawyer admitted that even the Samaritan and Jew might be neighbors; though he could not make up his mind to say the word "Samaritan," and preferred to phrase it, "He that showed mercy on him."

Thus, at another time, when the woman came to the house where Jesus was dining with Simon the Pharisee, and Simon was scandalized at the Master's allowing a sinful woman to touch him,—Jesus, by a story, showed Simon how the consciousness of sin might create a power of affection, deeper than could grow up in the heart of self-satisfied virtue.

When fault was found with him for healing on the sabbath, he put a question which silenced, if it did not convince, the captious formalist. It silenced him, and it may have convinced others. "You pull your ox out of a pit on the Sabbath: may not I pull out a man?"

Other cases of this kind will readily occur to the reader, in which Jesus, by means of questions, either made his meaning clear, silenced objection, or confuted his opponents by making them confute themselves.

(*c*) His evident aversion to verbal profession, and too easy assent to his claims.

"Good Teacher," began one. "Why do you call me good?" he replied; "Is any finite, human goodness worth considering, in the presence of the infinite goodness? The little goodness we possess is not ours: it is God's." So, at least, I interpret his words.

"Why do you call me Lord, instead of doing the things I teach?" said he, at another time. And yet there are many to-day who think it wrong not to be continually repeating the name of Christ,—at the end of their prayers, and in all their sermons. A certain divine found fault with the proclamation for thanksgiving of the great war-governor of Massachusetts, because "Christ" was not verbally mentioned in it. But God was mentioned repeatedly, and Christian duties and Christian piety were mentioned. Is the name of Christ to be regarded as a charm, or magical formula, more valuable than his truth or his spirit? Jesus did not think so.

In the days of Christ, as now, there was a class of persons who believed too easily, and needed to be made to see it. They were ready to accept every thing he said, at once, and praise it all. This sort of ready verbal assent was by no means satisfactory to him.

A woman once interrupted the course of his teaching by uttering a hosannah to his mother, and saying what a happy woman she must be to have such a son. He replied that he rather considered those happy who listened to God's word, and then obeyed it. The Roman-Catholic church has never learned that lesson; but, to this hour, spends more time in chanting "Blessed Virgin Mary!" than in hearing the truth of Jesus and doing it.

On another occasion Jesus was advising his hearers, when they gave a feast, to invite poor people and not rich ones. (This passage seems to have been very much overlooked by modern Christians, who invite to their parties party-giving people; their object being to get into society, or stay in it.) Some one in the crowd probably thought the subject was not sufficiently religious, and had a tendency toward "mere morality." So he called out, in the sonorous accent of self-satisfied piety, "Blessed is he that shall eat bread in the kingdom of God!" Whereupon Jesus told a story, the point of which was that many persons who believed that they wished above all else to see the kingdom of heaven would not like it very much when it came.

In like manner, he said to Nicodemus, "I am afraid you cannot see the kingdom of heaven, Nicodemus: a man must be made over and become all new, must be converted and be like a little child, to see the real kingdom of heaven. Peter saw it in a transient glimpse, a momentary vision; but I am afraid you cannot." Nicodemus came to expound a theory of the Messianic kingdom. He explained how he could believe, on grounds of logic, that Jesus was a divinely appointed teacher, because he worked miracles. But Jesus did not desire to have any one believe in him on that ground, or in that way. What he desired was that they should see and enter into the true kingdom of God. To do this, it was necessary to be child-like, pure in heart, poor in spirit; in short, to become new creatures, through and through, by seeing all things in a new way.

Popularity did not deceive him. When multitudes followed him, he turned and said, "If any man come after me, let him deny himself, and take up his cross." When the multitudes were shouting hosannah, tears came into his eyes at the sight of the city all of whose tendencies were toward self-destruction.

So Jesus taught. He argued from the Old Testament, quoting the example of David to show that the sabbath need not be kept as strictly as they believed. He quoted the example of Elisha to show that he had a right to go to those outside the Jewish pale. He refused to be umpire in matters not belonging to his mission. "Who made me a divider over you?" said he. So now, when we say, "Master, speak to the geologists that they shall not set aside the Mosaic account of the creation;" Jesus might reply, "That does not concern me or my religion at all: that belongs to science." Sometimes he taught by silence, as when he looked down and wrote on the ground, not wishing to make it too hard for the accusers, by looking at them while they went out. He left the bridge standing, for the flying enemy to escape by. To the captious Pharisee and Sadducee, he sometimes refused to speak; but to the poor Samaritan woman he taught the highest and holiest truths of the gospel. He did not believe that she was too ignorant or too corrupt to understand the great doctrine of the spirituality of God. To any open soul, he would teach any truth.

Another objection of the critics is, that Jesus was not original. He said what had been said before. By searching through all old religions and philosophies, it has been found that Confucius taught something like the Golden Rule; that in the Talmud are some sayings like those of the sermon on the mount; that if we put together what Pythagoras and Seneca, the Vedas and Zoroaster, Plato and Socrates, Antoninus and Epictetus have said, we shall find very many of the teachings of Jesus anticipated, — some here, some there. Granted. What then? Jesus did not profess to have invented truth, I suppose. If, when you have gathered all the wisest sayings of the wisest men, you find that Jesus said the same things, it shows that his teachings accord with human nature in its noblest aspirations. But if it all had been taught before, how happens it that it took such hold of the world when Jesus said it? If it were an old story, how could it revolutionize human history, and change the face of nations? Why did it only create new thought in the minds of philosophers when uttered by Plato, and create new life in the hearts of mankind when coming from Jesus? That is the question. It was because it came as a speculation in the one case, but as a reality in the other. It was because it was not from the surface thought, but from the depth of the soul. The originality which is of consequence, does not consist in the novelty of what is said, but in its vitality; and that depends on the depth from which it springs. When Jesus spoke, what he said came from those depths in the soul, where man stands face to face with God, with nature, with universal law, with the awful realities of time and eternity. It was no mere intellectual novelty he produced, with which to amuse men's intellects; but immortal truths, to live and work for all time. So he taught, as one having authority, and not as the Scribes.

If it be objected to our faith in Jesus, that the criticisms of the present time have made his history uncertain, and shaken our confidence in the authenticity of the Gospels, I reply that the truth of the gospel history of Jesus does not rest on critical reasons, nor can it be shaken by critical objections. It rests on the harmony and consent of the various accounts of this great person, from which evermore emerges that sublime figure, bearing all the authentic lineaments of reality. The human mind has the power of seeing what is true to nature, even though it be above all nature elsewhere observed. You might just as well look at the sun and doubt its reality, as read the story of Jesus and question its historic truth. All critical objections dissolve in air, before that divine face which looks out upon us from these simple records, through all the intervening centuries. It is the face of one whom we have learned to know better than our neighbors in the next street, better than the brother who sat with us by our father's fireside. Notwithstanding the narrowness of his nation, the ignorance of his biographers, the hardness of the age, the low views of God and man prevailing around him, we hear a voice which speaks with the astonishing authority of perfect insight, — a voice which creates a new era, which pours light on time and eternity. It is a voice so strong, yet so tender; so bold, yet so careful; so unhesitating in its absolute assurance, yet so condescending to all human weakness, ignorance, and sin, — that it sinks into our soul, needing no other proof of its reality than itself. Some things prove themselves to be true, and need no other evidence. So it is with the character of Jesus.

And might we not expect, from the nature of God, that he would give us such a revelation of his truth and love, as we find in Jesus Christ? "What man is there among you, being a father, who, when his son asks for bread, will he give him a stone?" For thousands of years, men's hearts have been feeling after God, asking him for this living bread. They have been looking for God in the magnificence of the rising sun; in the solemnity of the starry night; in the inscrutable beauty of air, fire, water; in the solitudes of the forests, and the mysterious and inaccessible mountains. Will not the Father come to these children who are seeking for him in all these ways? He comes; by the voices of sages, prophets, wise and good teachers, in all lands and times. But at last a Teacher arrives, who spake as man never spake, and before whose voice all other voices are hushed and still. He takes humanity by the hand, and leads it to an Infinite Father, to a holy law of eternal right, to a hope full of immortality. Does it not accord with the providence of God, that just such a teacher should be given to man? And shall we not say that he came, not by the will of the flesh or the will of man, but by the will of the loving Father of us all? The result has been, that, wherever Christianity has gone, men have become wiser, better, stronger. Christian nations are not what they should be; but, led by Christ, they are the leaders of the race. Is this an accident? Or is it not a part of the great plan of history? And do we not see that God's providence is eminently present in this greatest event of time, — the coming of Jesus of Nazareth into the world; that this has given a unity to all modern civilization; has made life everywhere new; has created a new heaven and a new earth? Jesus is to-day the Leader of the race. Is it reasonable or not, to believe that God meant him so to be?

I outgrow many teachers, but I find that I have not

outgrown Christ. I come to see more and more of truth in him every day. The words of his which I could not understand, I now understand better. His truth seems to me, every day, to be more deep, more high, more all-embracing, more soul-satisfying. The more we study and obey him, the more it becomes our truth and life. If we do his will, we know of the doctrine whether it be of God. So that Jesus is our Master and Teacher, by the same law of our nature as that by which others are; only fully, absolutely, and constantly. Other teachers are exhausted: his words are inexhaustible. The words of others at last grow cold and empty: his are spirit and life, always vital in every part. It is this which qualifies him to be the Teacher of the human race for ever, and his religion to be the universal religion of mankind. He asks us to be his disciples, and take him for our Teacher. He does not ask blind assent, but intelligent conviction. Our faith leads to sight. He also asks us to be his servants, and take him for Master. But he does not demand slavish service, but willing obedience. His service is perfect freedom. The condition of being his disciples as of being scholars anywhere, is faith; confidence in him as a good and wise teacher. This confidence makes us docile, ductile; attentive to his word; patient to wait, when we cannot immediately comprehend him. It makes us expectant of truth, with minds open to influence; receptive and not shut up; not hardened in our own dogmas and prejudices, but seeking for truth evermore. So at last, and only so, can we come to comprehend with all saints, what is the length and breadth and depth and height of this gospel of Jesus, and know the love of Christ, which passeth knowledge.

And now that we have considered some of these recent criticisms upon Christianity, what do they all amount to? They arise from an ignorance of the nature of Christianity, the nature of man, and the law of historic progress. They assume that human nature is naturally depraved, and incapable of rising to such a height of sublime and perfect beauty as we find in Jesus. They treat religion as though it were a speculation, set afloat by some human brain, and which can be planted here or there by the will of man; not as a grand providential upward movement, step by step, of the human race. And they treat Christianity as though it were the teaching of certain religious and moral truths, and do not see that it is the life of Christ himself, prolonged from age to age. They do not see that Christ is with us always, even to the end of the world; not as a speculation, but as a living influence; and that the real Christian is not one who believes a creed about Jesus, but one who receives his truth with an open mind, obeys his law with a glad heart, and is fed inwardly out of his life, evermore.

THIRD STEP.

FROM ROMANISM TO PROTESTANTISM.

"And call no man your father upon the earth: for one is your Father, which is in heaven." — *Matt.* xxiii. 9.

"But when Peter was come to Antioch, I withstood him to the face, because he was to be blamed." — *Galatians* ii. 11.

CHAPTER I.

The Idea of Romanism and of Protestantism.

WE now begin a new series of questions. We have compared atheism with theism, and find ourselves theists. This was our first step upward. We have next compared theism outside of Christianity, with Christian theism, and find the last an advance on the other; so that, in the interest of human progress, we have accepted Christian theism as an advance on deism. But now we see before us two forms of Christianity. One is called Romanism, the other, Protestantism. The first places supreme authority in the church, in the outward organization; the other, in the human soul. Which of these is an advance on the other?

When we accept Christianity as our law of life, we have certain intellectual questions to answer. Two of these become of great importance. The first concerns the source, the second the criterion of Christianity. "Where shall I find Christianity?" "How shall I distinguish the true from the false Christianity?" These are the questions which divide the Roman-

Catholic Church from all Protestant Churches, — divide them radically and fundamentally. Here is the principle of divergence, the source of all other differences. We begin, therefore, by the consideration of the respective principles of the two forms of Christianity.

When the question is asked, "Where shall I go to find Christianity?" the Protestant Churches reply, "To the Bible." "This," they say, "is the only infallible rule of faith and practice;" meaning, however, the only infallible source of belief, theoretical and practical. The Roman Catholic replies, "To the Bible and tradition." If I then ask, "Where shall I find tradition?" he replies, "In the church and its decisions." Just as actual law consists, not merely of statute law, but also of common law; not merely of laws as passed by the legislature, but also as these are interpreted by the decisions of successive courts of justice, — so, according to the Catholics, Christianity is made up of the truths of the Bible, not as we can take them from the Bible by personal study, but as they are explained to us by the fathers, the councils, and the popes. The other question concerns the criterion of truth. In a case of doubt as to what is Christian faith, who shall decide? The Catholic says, "The church shall decide for you." The Protestant says, "You must decide for yourself."

The Romanist, being asked for the source of Christianity, replies, "The Scriptures and tradition:" the

Protestant answers, "The Scriptures only." The Romanist being asked for the criterion of Christianity, replies, "The church;" the Protestant answers, "Private judgment."

This is the issue between the two bodies, as regards their fundamental speculative principle.

The Roman-Catholic theory is, that when Jesus completed the work of redemption by his death, and had risen, he founded a church, or society of believers, which was a regularly organized and corporate body, consisting of laity and clergy. The clergy, again, consisted of three orders, — bishops, priests, and deacons; and at the head of all, was placed Peter, with supreme power, as chief bishop and president of the whole body. To him and his successors Jesus gave the keys of the kingdom of heaven, and made him his vicar or viceroy, — king of the church below, as Christ himself was King above. Outside of the church, thus constituted, there is no salvation; because this church alone has authority to teach the truth, and administer the sacraments. Any one remaining in communion with this church is safe from eternal punishment: any one outside of it is liable to eternal punishment.

To us, children of the Puritans, Protestants of the Protestants; born under a system which teaches us from childhood that it is a duty to seek the truth, think for ourselves, and search the Scriptures independently, — it seems strange that such an enormous claim should be allowed by any reasonable person. We have been in the habit of thinking the Roman-Catholic Church so opposed to the spirit of the age, the progress of civilization, and the public opinion of the world, that it must soon come to an end. But, in saying this, we underrate the forces which sustain this great institution. The Roman-Catholic Church is still an immense power in the world, for good or evil, probably for both. We shall never conquer it by assuming that its time is past, or by ignoring its power. It is stronger to-day than it was in the sixteenth century. It makes more proselytes from Protestantism by argument and direct influence, than Protestantism from it. It concedes nothing, refuses all compromise, adds new dogmas to the old, and replies to the public opinion of the world by calm defiance. Nearly a thousand bishops and prelates, summoned from all parts of the world, are now in Rome, by command of the Pope. No congress, parliament, or national assembly on earth, wields any such power as is to-day in the hands of this great council. If it declares the infallibility of the pope, that doctrine must be accepted by nearly one hundred and fifty millions of persons, or they must cease to be Catholics. It is not merely among an ignorant people that this church rules. Here, in America, it is steadily advancing. It has the largest churches, the most imposing cathedrals, the best organized hospitals, growing up in every part of the country. In Boston and in

Milwaukee, in San Francisco and New Orleans, it is taking possession of the best situations, erecting the noblest buildings, accumulating funds, making proselytes. While Protestant sects are contending with each other, and disputing; working without concord, each for itself, — this thoroughly organized body is doing the same work in the Arctic Zone, and the tropics. It is actuated by one idea, — that of conquering all opponents. It boasts itself able to put down our free institutions, take possession of our public schools, and re-establish on this continent the power it has been losing in the old. It changes nothing, improves nothing. It refuses to adopt any of the ideas of the nineteenth century, or any of the discoveries of science which may conflict with its past and present opinions. It offers a frank defiance to the whole spirit of American institutions; to the free press, free schools, free inquiry, free thought, freedom of conscience. The pope, in his Syllabus, declares it a grave error to say that the civil government ought not to put down heresy by force. If Rome gets the power in this country, no reason can be given why she should not re-establish the Inquisition, and burn heretics at the stake. If she thought it right to do this in the sixteenth century, as she does not change her opinions, she must think it right to do it in the nineteenth; whenever she has the power and finds it expedient. She wishes to establish, here in America, the system of monasteries and nunneries which many of the Catholic nations of Europe have abolished. She will make use of our religious freedom to build up her power; and then she will try to destroy our religious freedom. That is her expectation, her determination, her purpose. I do not mean to say that all Roman Catholics are opposed to religious freedom, or in favor of persecution; but the power which to-day governs the church, — the Company of Jesus, — has no reluctance, no hesitation, in so determining. If this Society triumph at Rome, in the Ecumenical Council, their power will be absolute in the church, and no element there can resist them.

It is a mistake made, almost universally, by Protestants, to regard the declaration of papal infallibility by the Vatican Council as a mere theoretical assertion of impossible claims. Almost all Protestant writers are amused by it, and consider it as simply ridiculous. But we must not suppose that so sagacious a body as the Roman Curia have no important practical object in view in thus compelling the bishops to admit the infallibility of the pope. It means a great deal practically. It is simply changing a constitutional monarchy into an absolute despotism. The Company of Jesus has always been such a despotism. Every member of it has been a soldier, bound to obey every order of his superiors without question. The present plan is to virtually transform the whole Catholic Church into the Company of Jesus. The motto of the whole Catholic Church will then be "Perinde ac cadaver." Every bishop will be bound to control his diocese according to directions from Rome. A papal brief will then be like the order of the general of an army, to be obeyed absolutely, without hesitation, by every good Catholic.

> "Not theirs to make reply,
> Not theirs to reason why:
> Theirs but to do or die."

The plan is, by this magnificent centralization, to give to the whole Catholic Church the aggressive power which has made the Company of Jesus such splendid soldiers in the service of the pope. As a nation, in its hour of peril from internal rebellion or external foes, chooses a dictator, and puts the whole power in his hands; so the Catholic Church, perceiving how it is endangered by the advance of science and the spirit of the age, proposes to make the pope an absolute dictator.

The object is a practical one, and perfectly logical. The declaration of infallibility is placing a secure theoretical foundation for the exercise of this absolute power. When this has been once declared, the pope may, for example, forbid any Catholic children to go to schools, except such as are under the control of ecclesiastics of their own church. Any parent who disobeys, will then be liable to excommunication. He can only choose between obedience and leaving the church. And every Catholic knows that to leave the church is to expose himself to an amount of social abuse and persecution which very few are strong enough to resist.

The plan, then, is a fine piece of strategic wisdom. It is true that the bow may be so much bent as to break. A very possible result of carrying out this decree may be schism. It is quite possible, that it may produce independent national churches in France, Spain, Italy, Austria, or Germany. These bodies, retaining their church buildings, priests, liturgies, as at present, would by no means be objectionable to the great mass of Catholics. To them the church means their own priest, and their usual worship. So that without becoming Protestants, or perceiving any change, they might become independent of Rome and of the papacy.

But it is idle to disguise the fact, that there is a great conflict before us in this country, — not with Roman Catholics, nor with the Roman-Catholic Church considered as a religion, but with the power of that organization, as wielded by the Jesuits. To this compact, determined, relentless power, we Protestants present a scattered crowd of unorganized sects, a divided purpose, and an unsettled creed. Not a Protestant Church is certain of its own opinions. In the sixteenth century Protestants could oppose to the infallibility of the church, the infallibility of the Bible. All Protestants believed in that then: how many believe in it now? As the Macedonian phalanx marched straight through the mob of Persian soldiers which called itself an army, so the Church of Rome, strong in its numbers and its union, laughs in derision at the divided sects of the Protestants, and anticipates a certain victory.

And its victory is certain, unless we have on our side one power which may essentially help us; and that is, TRUTH. In the sixteenth century, three hundred and fifty years ago, truth, without organization, without numbers, with no prestige, no popularity, — truth, uttered by the lips of a single man, Martin Luther, — shook all of Christendom to its centre, and overthrew Romanism through half of Europe. On the side of Rome are numbers, prestige, organization, union; on the other side, freedom and truth. If the claim of Rome is false, nothing can save it. When the foundations of a building are giving way, no buttresses against the walls can keep it from coming down.

The Roman-Catholic principle of authority, on which all else is founded, may be briefly summed up in these three principles: —

1. The Christian church is an outward, visible organization, founded by Christ, who made St. Peter its head, who transmitted his authority to his successors, the bishops of Rome. The Christian church consists of all those who are in communion with Rome and acknowledge the papal primacy, and of no others.

2. The Christian church, thus understood, is infallible, and protected against all errors by the Holy

Spirit. Its voice, therefore, when uttered, is the voice of God.

3. As no one can be saved except through Christ, and as no one can commune with Christ except through his church, it follows that outside of the church there is no salvation.

What are the arguments used in support of this immense assumption? A few texts of Scripture, and a few considerations taken from a presumed necessity or expediency. Christ said to Peter, "Upon this rock I will build my church." "And I will give unto thee the keys of the kingdom of heaven." He commanded him to feed his sheep. He told his disciples that he would be with them always, even to the end of the world. But the Protestant answer to these texts is, that the keys, as the expression of opening and shutting the gates of the kingdom, are also given to the other apostles (Matt. xviii. 18) and the power of forgiving sin communicated to them all (John xx. 23). It is also argued that the meaning of Jesus was that his church was to be built on the confession of Peter, not on Peter himself, since he presently calls Peter "Satan;" since the church was actually built on the confession, and was not built on Peter; and it is declared that no other foundation can be laid than that which is laid, which is Jesus Christ (1 Cor. iii. 11). Christians are said to be built upon the foundation of apostles and prophets, Jesus Christ himself being the chief corner-stone (Eph. ii. 20). Peter, therefore, was not the head of the church, nor even the foundation of the church in any exclusive sense. But on account of his energy, and the personal conviction which animated him in his confession of Christ, Peter was made for the moment the representative of all the apostles. But if Peter was distinguished by Christ as a leader among his brethren, he received no authority over them. For this Jesus nowhere has said; and he surely would have declared it, if this had been as essential a feature of Christianity as the Roman-Catholic doctrine assumes. He was once distinctly asked by his disciples who would be the greatest in his kingdom. He does not tell them that Peter is to be the greatest, but rebukes them for the very thought that one should be superior to the other (Matt. xviii. 1). On another occasion, (Matt. xx. 20–28), he taught the same lesson. There is no evidence in the Book of Acts that Peter was regarded as superior in any sense to the other apostles. But, admitting that Peter possessed any such primacy, there is nothing to show that it was more than personal, depending on his individual character, and incapable of being transmitted to any successors. Admitting that it was capable of transmission, it has still to be proved that the bishops of Rome are the successors of Peter. It is possible that he may have been at Rome, though there is no evidence to that effect in the New Testament. He was in Jerusalem as late as A.D. 52 (Acts xv.); then in Antioch (Gal. ii. 11); also in Babylon (1 Peter v. 13).

Neither of his two epistles speak of any residence in Rome. The Apostle Paul, in his epistle to the Romans, does not salute Peter as bishop of that church, nor even mention his name. Afterward, when Paul goes to Rome (Acts xxviii.), he does not find Peter there. An ancient tradition, indeed (Ignatius in Epist. ad Romanos; Eusebius ii. 25; Irenæus, Adv. Hær. iii. 1, 3), mentions his martyrdom at Rome, A.D. 67. That he was a bishop there, is first stated by Jerome. Though Eusebius (iii. 1, 2) mentions Peter's preaching in Pontus, Galatia, Bithynia, Cappadocia, Asia, and lastly in Rome, where he was crucified, he says nothing of his having been bishop there. He rather intimates that Linus was the first bishop "after the martyrdom of Paul and Peter." Irenæus also says plainly that the holy apostles Peter and Paul founded the Roman church, and made Linus its bishop. The Apostolic Constitutions (vii. 46) say that of the church of Rome Linus was the first bishop, ordained by Paul; and Clement, after Linus's death, ordained by Peter.

But though we grant that Peter was made head of the church, that he was in Rome, and that he was bishop there, this does not prove at all that the bishops of Rome have inherited his primacy or his authority. His authority was that of an inspired apostle, taught by Jesus himself, and a witness of his resurrection. The bishops of Rome, since the time of Peter, have had none of these claims to respect.

And even if the bishops of Rome are successors of

Peter, this does not prove their infallibility, or the infallibility of the church. Peter was not infallible himself; how could he transmit infallibility? He was wrong in the course he took at Antioch, and gravely erred, so as to be rebuked by Paul, and charged with dissimulation (Gal. ii. 11.) The result was the same, whether his error here was intellectual or moral: his conduct gave a false impression of Christianity. He taught dangerous error by his actions. If he was intellectually infallible, such infallibility was of no use, since it did not prevent him from teaching false doctrine by his conduct.

The principal arguments, however, relied upon to prove the infallibility of the church, are derived from the desirableness, advantage, or necessity of such a power. In this way Moehler (Symbolism, § xxxvii.) argues that the church is infallible, because it ought to be so. "Every believer," he says, "must bestow his whole confidence upon her; and she must therefore merit the same. Giving himself up to her guidance, he ought, in consequence, to be secured against delusion: she must be inerrable." In like manner, Mr. O. A. Brownson has argued that the true church of Christ is, and must be, an authoritative and infallible body of pastors and teachers. His reasons are, that to be saved one must be a Christian; to be a Christian, one must believe in Christianity; that this belief must be verbal, having for its object distinct propositions;

that these may be misunderstood, and so need an infallible interpreter to explain them.

The Protestant answer to this train of argument is as follows: —

If human salvation depends on belonging to any particular outward organization, this would certainly be distinctly stated in the New Testament. Jesus nowhere tells us that his church is that which is to be in communion with Peter and his successors, that this church will be endowed with infallibility, or that outside of it there is no salvation.

On the contrary, all that Jesus says, in regard to human salvation, indicates that it is personal and not organic, — mediated indeed, as we have seen, through other lives, but not bound up with any external corporation, organization, mode of worship, or church connection. The Samaritan woman raised the question which was the true church, that of the Jews, or that of the Samaritans. Jesus replied that neither was the true church, as far as true worship was concerned; that true worship was worshipping in spirit and in truth, not according to the Jewish or the Samaritan ritual. He knew nothing, taught nothing, of worship localized at Jerusalem or at Rome. He does not say, "He that communes with me through Peter and his successors, he it is that loveth me;" but, "He that hath my commandments, and keepeth them, he it is that loveth me." He does not say, "This is life eternal, to receive the sacraments at the hands of the true priesthood;" but,

"This is life eternal, that they might know Thee, the only true God, and Jesus Christ, whom thou hast sent." He does not say, "Blessed are those who belong to the true church;" but, "Blessed are the pure in heart." Now, if Jesus knew and intended that salvation was only possible by means of union with a certain outward organization, can it be that he should never once have mentioned that fact? This, of itself, is sufficient to refute the audacious claim of any visible church to be the only avenue to Christ and to heaven.

Again: if our salvation depends on our belonging to the true church, our salvation depends on our ability to discover it. Amid the conflict of sects and parties, we must be able to find our way through the intricacies of controversy, the plausibility of opposing arguments, and the difficulty of learned investigation. Mr. Brownson, in the fervor of his conversion to the Roman-Catholic Church, published an argument in its behalf; reduced, as he believed, to its simplest form. This argument occupied sixty pages of his review, and consisted of a chain of propositions, any one of which failing, the whole would go to the ground. Is it possible that God has made the salvation of his creatures depend upon the possession of such a logical acumen, and trained intellect, as shall enable them properly to weigh such arguments as these? Is this the gospel which is hidden from the wise and prudent, and revealed unto babes?

I have before me a volume called, "Evidence for the

Papacy," by the Hon. Colin Lindsay, published in 1870. It contains, "the grounds which led to his conversion to the Catholic Church." The author says he devoted more than six months' incessant study to the question, before he was brought to the conclusion that he ought to become a Roman Catholic. He was an intelligent and educated man, who had already studied the history of Christianity, and had some leanings toward Rome. Now if it takes six months of conscientious study, to enable such a man to see clearly the argument in favor of the Roman Church, how is it possible for the great mass of men ever to become Catholics, honestly and from clear conviction? But if they do not become so, they are outside of Christianity, and outside of the way of salvation.

It is argued that an infallible guide is necessary, in order to prevent men from going astray, and that, therefore, Jesus established the Roman-Catholic Church as such a guide. This argument assumes that the New Testament is so obscure a book, that we cannot learn from it the way to God and heaven, unless we have an infallible guide to show us how to interpret it. But Jesus did not represent the way to heaven as so mysterious as this. On one occasion he was asked this very question, "Master, what shall I do to inherit eternal life?" He made the inquirer answer his own question, Love God, and love your neighbor. This Jesus declared to be the right answer. But if it is true that, in order to love God and our neighbor, we must belong to the true church; and that to find out which is the true church, we must be able to study ecclesiastical history and sift a complicated argument, — then the lawyer's answer was not the right one. What he had to do to inherit eternal life, was, in the first place to join the true church, and become one of Christ's disciples.

One argument, often dwelt upon, to show the necessity of an infallible church, is, that we need some certain assurance of truth. We need an infallible authority to lean upon, in order to be at rest from doubt and uncertainty in matters of religion. But this argument would seem to show that we ought also to have an infallible guide to show us the way into the infallible church. For whether is it easier to understand the words of Jesus, or to understand the arguments in behalf of the Church of Rome? If we cannot understand the sermon on the mount, or the parable of the Good Samaritan, without an infallible church to explain them to us, still less can we find our way through the tangled thicket of the Roman-Catholic and Protestant argument without some infallible guide to show us which is right. This simple consideration, we are bold to say, is a sufficient answer to the whole argument for the necessity of an infallible church. If an infallible church is necessary, an infallible guide to the infallible church is still more necessary. Nor does the difficulty stop here. We shall also need an infallible witness to the infallible guide. We shall then need an infallible proof of the infallibility of the witness to the infallible guide into the infallible church. There is plainly no end to this chain of necessities. Every argument which goes to show the necessity of an infallible church, shows also the necessity of an infinite succession of infallibilities to direct us to it.

But suppose this difficulty somehow obviated, and that we are at last safely arrived within the infallible church. We have now a living witness to explain the truth to us, and make us understand what it is. But here comes a new difficulty. In receiving this truth, is our mind to be active or passive? Is it to consider it, understand it, express it in forms adapted to its own habits of thought; or is it merely to receive it passively, without thinking about it at all? In other words, are we to try to see the truth of the proposition; or are we to assent to its terms, even though they seem to us to be false? If the first, if the mind is to be active, then it is plain that the infallibility instantly disappears. Infallible truth falling into a fallible mind, and arranged, according to its own fallible judgment, in fallible human language, loses its infallible character. This, the Roman Church sees so clearly, that it does not require conviction, but only assent. It does not wish active thought, but only passive submission. It knows well that we cannot believe by being told to believe. It therefore only requires that we should assent to the truth of what is told us. But if what is told us seems to us to be false, then to assent to its truth is equivalent to telling a falsehood. In requiring assent to its doctrines, the Church of Rome deliberately places a lie at the foundation of its whole system. The first duty of a man, in order to go to heaven, is to tell a lie. It is to say that he believes what he does not believe; to give assent where there is no conviction; to promise to seem to accept what in his soul he denies: in short, to believe with his will, and not with his intellect. This is the root-falsehood in the Roman-Catholic system, which poisons it all the way through. This takes out of it simple honesty, truthfulness, solid conviction, and vitiates the whole system. And in thus demanding assent instead of conviction, it is curious and tragic to see that it contradicts the fundamental text on which its whole system rests. When Jesus told Peter that he would build his church on "this rock," it was because, in his declaration of faith in Christ, he had not said what "flesh and blood had revealed" unto him, but what his Heavenly Father had shown. That is, the conviction which made Peter a rock was his own interior sight of the truth, and not a mere outward assent to the statement of another. It was not a hearsay belief, which flesh and blood had revealed, but a sight of truth which God revealed to him. Those who call themselves Peter's successors reverse Peter's method, and ask us to believe in "flesh and blood" communications, and not the inspirations of the Spirit in our own souls.

See, then, to what a curious result we have arrived.

The *ecclesia docens*, or teaching church, does not, as it seems, teach at all. It merely commands. "Sic volo, sic jubeo; stat pro ratione voluntas." An infallible church might, one would suppose, teach infallibly. It ought to convince the understanding, clear away difficulties, remove doubts, pour a flood of light into the intellect, and make, not obedient servants, but clear-sighted friends. So did Jesus teach, as we have seen in the previous chapters. He said, "Henceforth I call you not servants, for the servant knoweth not what his lord doeth: but I have called you friends; for all things that I have heard of my Father I have made known unto you." Nor did the apostles ask for any blind submission, though clothed with apostolic authority. They told their disciples to prove all things, to retain what was good; to abstain from whatever appeared to be evil; not to believe every spirit, but to try the spirits. They let their light shine. When Paul found those at Corinth who did not believe in the resurrection of the dead, he did not order them to retract their opinion and submit to his authority, but argued with them, in order to convince them.

For such reasons as these, we, as Protestants, reject the fundamental principle of the Roman-Catholic Church. We do not find any such authority conferred by Christ. We do not find any such church established in the New Testament. We do not perceive its necessity, its advantage, or its expediency.

On the contrary, it seems to us at war with the principles of the gospel, and the nature of the human mind. It enslaves the soul, and teaches it to falsify its own instincts. It teaches that God is better pleased with insincere conformity, than with honest dissent; that he prefers passive submission to active and growing conviction.

No doubt much of this evil principle still remains in the Protestant Churches. As Milton says, "This iron yoke of outward conformity hath left a slavish print upon our necks: the ghost of a linen decency still haunts us." Protestants also are satisfied if men will assent to an orthodox creed: whether they believe it or not, is of much smaller consequence. But, in this, Protestants are inconsistent with their fundamental principle of private judgment. The logic of that principle, therefore, will gradually but surely lead them to perfect freedom of thought. But the Church of Rome has based itself upon the opposite principle. Its method is to repress inquiry, chain thought, and substitute everywhere assertion for honest inquiry. It holds itself justified in denying the plainest facts of history when they seem injurious to the church. Pious falsehoods have long been favorite weapons in its armory. Many Catholic writers are indeed pure from this stain. But the tendency in the church is not to throw it off, but to retain it, and to intensify it. So long as the Jesuits rule in Rome, so long will Jesuitism pervade the church with its detestable spirit.

The magnificent success of Protestantism in the sixteenth century was checked in the seventeenth. It was then arrested, and never renewed. This was perhaps owing to two errors. The first error of Protestantism consisted in making the Scripture the only source of faith and practice. It did this because it wanted an infallible standard of faith to oppose to the infallibility of the Roman Church. It adopted this doctrine as a matter of expediency, as a war-cry; and also, because the heart of man cries out for something outwardly solid to stand on. It could not have an infallible church, so it took an infallible Bible. This was well as long as men believed the Bible to be infallible. But the conscientious study of the Scripture revealed in it contradictions and difficulties: nothing then seemed to remain firm. Protestantism ought to have said: "There is no infallible source of Christian knowledge; no outward infallibility possible or desirable. The Bible, human history, the soul itself, Christian experience, reason, — all are sources of Christian knowledge, but none are infallible, nor were meant to be."

The other mistake, more important still in its consequences than the first, was the actual abandonment of the second principle of Protestantism; viz., the Right of Private Judgment. The Protestant Church, having taken the ground of Private Judgment, ought to have encouraged men to judge for themselves, no matter what results they arrived at. They ought not to say, "Judge, but come to our conclusions, else we shall exclude you." This showed a want of trust in Christianity itself. They should have said, "Let men go to Christ, and then all will be safe."

Whenever Protestantism does this, becoming true to its own principle, it will once more go forward. Then it will again become a mighty advancing Power, with "many members, but one body." Then it will have a variety in unity, and a unity in variety. It will then accept all the good in the Roman-Catholic Church; all the truth in all heresies; all the good outside of Christianity, in heathen religions. It will become large, deep, high, and advancing, as it was in the beginning.

The day is to come in which there is to be a truly Catholic Church, which shall include Roman organization and Protestant freedom, — shall include all who call themselves Christians and who love the Lord Jesus Christ in sincerity. This will be the true Coming of Christ. When this great day arrives, all the ancient prophecies will be fulfilled. Then wrong will cease, the sword be beaten into a ploughshare, the cow and the bear feed together, and a little child lead them. Then the world will be converted to Christianity; and Christians, loving each other, will be able to make the world believe that God has sent their Master to be its leader and its guide to Him.

CHAPTER II.

The Doctrines of the Roman-Catholic Church.

IN our last chapter we criticised the fundamental idea of the Roman-Catholic Church. We shall next consider the doctrinal systems of Romanism and Protestantism. We first examined the sources and tests of truth, or the authority of the church and of reason. We have now to look at the two methods of salvation as indicated by the two systems respectively.

The great question of practical religion is this: How shall a man be just before God? or, to use a more modern phraseology, How does goodness come? And there are two answers. The first is, Let a man do good, and he will become good. Let him begin by doing all the good he can, and he will be able to do more. Goodness will work in from the surface to the centre. Good actions will produce good motives. He that is faithful in the least will, by and by, become faithful in much. He who employs well his single talent will, by and by, have more. Faithfulness will lead to faith: good conduct will at last create a good heart. And hence the formula of the Apostle James: "Man is justified by works, and not by faith only."

The other answer is exactly opposite. It says, 'If one wishes to do good, he must first become good. Out of the heart are the issues of life. It takes a good tree to bring forth good fruit. Until the heart is right, it is impossible to do any thing really right; when the heart is right, it is impossible to do any thing really wrong. He that is born of God does not commit sin. Goodness works out from the centre to the circumference: the soul makes the body, not the body the soul. Good motives will produce good actions. Faith results in fidelity: a good heart creates a good life. And hence the formula of the Apostle Paul: "We conclude that man is justified by faith, without the deeds of the law."

Which of these methods is the true one? The answer of common sense, and of experience, is that both are true. Every time one does a good action it makes him a better man. Every thing which purifies the heart leads to better actions. And therefore, at first, both methods prevailed in the Christian Church. Faith and works were accounted the two wings with which the soul flies upward to God. But with the division of the church in the sixteenth century, each section adopted and intensified one of these principles. Protestant theology said we are saved by faith only. Catholic theology said we are saved by sacraments. And this constitutes the vital, fundamental distinction between the doctrinal systems of the two churches.

Orthodox Protestant theology declares that until a

man is inwardly converted and changed all his best acts are odious in the sight of God. His noblest virtues are splendid vices. To try to make himself better by doing his duties, or by practising works of charity, is to deceive himself. To such extremes, and to such fatal antinomianism has Protestant theology often gone, wholly misunderstanding and exaggerating Paul's doctrine.

Meantime, the Roman-Catholic Church has gone to the opposite extreme, and has taught that we are saved by outward sacraments. These sacraments are seven: baptism, confirmation, the eucharist, penance, extreme unction, holy orders, and matrimony. By each of these a supernatural grace is infused into the soul. When the outward action is performed in the right way, the inward result follows of necessity. The only condition is that the priest shall intend to perform it aright. Thus in the time of Pope Nicholas I., a Jew baptized the Bulgarians for money; and the pope declared their baptism valid. In the time of Pope Innocent IX., some Saracens, who did not even know what the Christian Church was, performed baptism, and the pope declared that also to be valid baptism. The whole virtue lay in the external act, apart from the motives of those concerned.*

The theory of the Catholic Church is that by baptism original sin is removed and spiritual life is com-

* Hase, Handbuch der Protestantischen Polemik, p. 377.

municated to the soul.* He who dies without being baptized goes to hell: he who is baptized, and then dies, goes to heaven. Thus the mercy of God is made to depend on the carelessness or thoughtfulness of a nurse, or a mother. If the mother forgets the baptism, or puts off the baptism, and the child falls sick and dies, God is unable to save it; if the mother re-

---

* Thomas Aquinas has four questions upon baptism, each containing several sections. The first question concerns the form; the second, Who ought to administer it? the third, Who ought to receive it? the fourth, What are the effects? Under the last, he says that all sins are removed by baptism, and all guilt before God, proceeding from original sin. By baptism he teaches that one is delivered from eternal punishment, and obtains the beatific vision, but is not delivered from the temporal punishment due to sin. The Council of Trent anathematized those who said that baptism was not necessary to salvation. The Roman Catechism declares that the faithful must be taught that all men are born subject to eternal misery, from which they can only be saved by being baptized. It also declares that there is no way of safety for children except through baptism. Bellarmine asserts that the church has always believed that infants, departing from this life without being baptized, must perish. Moehler says that, according to Catholic doctrine, original sin in children, in adults original sin together with actual sins, is by the due reception of baptism removed. See Thom. Aq. Summa, P. iii. qu. 66, &c. Canons and decrees of the Council of Trent, can. 3, 4, 5. Catechismus Romanus, ii. 2, 34. Moehler, Symbolism, chaps. 28, 32. Roman theologians usually place the substance of baptism in the application of water, the use of the baptismal formula, and the intention to baptize by him who administers it.

members and has the child baptized, God is obliged to save it. Thus baptism is turned into a charm, a piece of magic, by which a power is exercised over the Deity, without any relation to morality or piety. Two missionaries, we will suppose, go into the heart of India or China. One devotes himself to teaching Christianity, and possibly succeeds in convincing a hundred persons of the truth of Christianity, but baptizes none of them. The other does not teach Christianity at all, but persuades a thousand mothers to let him baptize their children. They do not know what it means, but think it a pretty thing to have it done. According to the Roman-Catholic doctrine, the first missionary, who preaches the gospel, has not saved a single soul from hell; but the other, who merely baptized without teaching any thing, has saved a thousand.

This, as I said, is certainly making of baptism a magic ceremony. But this principle has been carried very far by Roman-Catholic missionaries. Xavier, the apostle to the Hindoos, baptized in one month ten thousand Indians at Travancore. It is evident that he could not have given them much knowledge of Christianity. The Jesuits sometimes baptized the Chinese secretly behind their backs; and one missionary himself says, that he carried with him always two bottles, one containing holy water, and the other a sweet-scented water. When the mothers brought him their sick children, he would put some of the fragrant fluid upon them to please the mothers, and then baptize them secretly with the other. All this is consistent with the theory that the child is saved by the outward act. But it is not very consistent with the Apostle Paul's saying: "I thank God I baptized none of you, except Crispus and Gaius, and perhaps the family of Stephen, and I think no others; for Christ sent me not to baptize, but to preach the gospel."

One result of making the value of Christianity depend on an outward act is to make all its details of great importance. If being baptized makes the difference between heaven and hell, it is very important to know exactly what baptism is. Accordingly, it has been carefully defined by Roman-Catholic theologians. It consists in three parts, (1) application of water, (2) repeating the formula, "I baptize thee," &c., (3) the intention to baptize, on the part of the person who performs it.

The question at one time arose (and very naturally) in the Catholic Church, How *much* water is necessary for valid baptism? For if an infant's salvation depends on its receiving Christian baptism, and if baptism is invalid which is wanting in either of the three constituents above mentioned, it is certainly highly important to know exactly how much water is necessary. It has always been the doctrine of Catholics that total immersion is not essential. How *little* water, then, is sufficient? Is the quantity of moisture which always adheres to the ends of the fingers enough? This, it is agreed, is not enough. Finally, it has been decided by the theologians that the smallest quantity sufficient for baptism is a drop of water which will run upon the face. Hence the difference between the salvation and everlasting damnation of an infant is the difference between a drop of water which will run, and a drop which will not. If, when the child was baptized, there was a drop applied to its face *which ran*, and the child dies, he is safe, and goes to heaven. If it did not run, and the child dies, he goes to hell.

Such views degrade the character of God to the level of the pagan deities, or Eastern genii, who can be controlled by the correct application of a charm. Religion and its sacraments are reduced to magical incantations. The soul is fed with external ceremonies instead of spiritual food. The tendency of such a sacramental salvation is to cause men to make clean the outside of the cup and the platter only.

Another important sacrament, in the Church of Rome, is that of penance. It consists of three parts: penitence, confession, and satisfaction.

All sins are either mortal or venial. A mortal sin is that which destroys in the soul the principle of life imparted by baptism, and leaves him who commits it again exposed to eternal damnation. The sacrament of penance then comes in, to restore the lost grace, and to renew the life of God in the soul. The first part of penance is sorrow for sin, and its consequences. But this sorrow (according to the Council of Trent,

Sess. xiv. Pœnit. c. 4) need not proceed from the love of God, but only from fear of hell. The second part of penance is confession, including absolution. According to the Decrees of Trent, confession must be made to a priest, at least once a year. The power of the priest to forgive sin is founded on the passages of Scripture (John xx. 22; Matt. xviii. 18), in which Jesus says to his disciples, "Receive the Holy Ghost. Whose soever sins ye remit, they are remitted to them, and whose soever sins ye retain, they are retained." "Whatsoever ye shall bind on earth shall be bound in heaven." But the Roman Church assumes, without proof, that Jesus gave his disciples this power as priests, and not as Christians. According to the Protestant view, every true Christian, just as far as he possesses genuine Christian experience, has the same power of binding and loosing which the apostles had. Every one who is in the spirit of truth and love can remit or retain sin. His words do not merely announce an official and formal forgiveness, but convey the essence of forgiveness to the soul. He speaks to the conscience and heart, as God speaks to them, because speaking from God's spirit in his own soul. When the weight of sin has been taken off our own soul by the spirit of God, we can take it from the soul of another. "He who is spiritual judgeth all things," says the apostle. The Roman Church, in limiting this power of forgiving sin to the priesthood, changes it from a spiritual power into an official act.

The power of absolution was not ascribed to the priesthood until the time of Thomas Aquinas. Till then the formula commonly used by the priest was, "I pray God to absolve thee;" afterward it became, "I absolve thee."* The Scripture says, "Confess your faults one to another;"† it does not say, "Confess to the priest." In the early church, confession of sin was made to the whole church, and auricular confession came afterward. Gieseler says ‡ that, until the twelfth century, the confession of private sins had not been considered an indispensable condition of forgiveness, and it was allowable to confess to a layman. It was first made obligatory to confess to a priest, once a year, by the Lateran Council, A.D. 1215.

No doubt there are advantages in auricular confession. It tends to prevent crime in those who still believe in the necessity of confessing, yet such persons are not those who usually commit crime. It frequently causes atonement, or restitution, to be made. It enables the priest to retain control over the rude masses; and this last is its chief advantage.

The Council of Trent declares that only *mortal* sins

---

* Thomas, Summa III., qu. 84, art. 3. "In quibusdam absolutionibus, absolvens non utitur oratione *indicitiva*, Ego te absolvo! sed oratione *deprecativa*, Misereatur vestri omnipotens Deus! vel Absolutionem tribuat vobis Omnipotens!"

† James v. 16.

‡ Vol. ii. p. 349 (Am. ed. Cunningham's translation).

need to be confessed. But as few Catholics know precisely the difference between mortal and venial sin, it is deemed safer to confess every thing.

The evils of auricular confession are so great, that they outweigh, by far, its advantages. It gives too much power to the priesthood, and maintains the baneful distinction between priest and people. It is used as the means of carrying out the arbitrary purposes of the Roman Curia. Thus, priests may be told not to give absolution to those parents who send their children to Protestant or secular schools.

One of the worst evils of auricular confession is the corruption of mind often produced by the priest's questions. Thoughts of evil, which never before existed in the soul, are conveyed there, unintentionally, by the confessor. The confessor studies the treatises put into his hands in the seminary, in which all sorts of sins are minutely described; and he is told that it is his duty to find out whether any of these have been committed. Fancy an innocent girl questioned as to every detail of her private life according to these manuals, so full of the filth gathered from the most corrupt practices of the foulest times! *

---

* In such a manual, not published in the Middle Ages, but in 1868, — not in Latin, but in French; not in Mexico, but in Paris, — we find all the details of lasciviousness carefully described, and directions like the following for the guidance of the confessor: "The confessor should appear, at first, mild and benevolent. He must persuade the young persons to tell with simplicity all they know on the point in question.

According to the Roman theology, venial sins need not be confessed, but are atoned for by various re-

---

He must not seem moved or astonished by any thing he hears, and he must not appear to listen with much curiosity or interest: he ought, in fact, to seem rather indifferent to the charges the penitents make against themselves. He may say that he has heard more on such subjects than they can tell him. In putting questions, he must be very careful to touch this dangerous subject lightly, and to use much prudence and reserve, so as not, by his very questions, to teach the penitents the evils which perhaps they are fortunately ignorant of."

"To detect bad habits, you must not seem to doubt their existence. Do not inquire concerning the essential fact, but concerning the accessory circumstances. Instead of asking if they have committed such or such a sin, which you fear they are concealing from you, you must make them say *how many times they have committed it.* If they hesitate to reply, name a large number, far beyond what is likely, so as to embolden them to confess a smaller number. In general, before they have finished speaking, begin to excuse them, throwing the blame on their accomplices, and saying that they probably would not have committed such improper acts if some corrupt companions had not taught them how, against their own wishes," &c.

"There is another important point. In speaking to females, married or otherwise, about this class of sins, the confessor should mention that he has obtained his information from medical books, &c. Otherwise they may suspect the priest of personal impurity, and such suspicions have been known to give rise to indecent, improper, and dangerous suggestions on the part of the penitents." — Mœchialogie: Traité des Péchés contre les Sixième et Neuvième Commandements du Décalogue, et de Toutes les Questions Matrimoniales, par le Père Debreyne. Quatrième edition. Paris: 1868.

ligious practices, such as repeating the Lord's Prayer, the use of holy water, manducation (that is, eating bread which has been blessed), being present at the mass, listening with reverence to the preaching, repeating the confession in the service, giving alms, and receiving the benediction of the priest. It will be seen that these are all quasi sacramental acts, and do not include any process of self-correction.

It is, however, also taught distinctly by the church of Rome, that, outside of its communion, there is no remission, either of original, mortal, or venial sin; for even to be forgiven venial sin, one must be in a state of grace.

The satisfaction contained in penance consists in the performance of such practices as may be commanded by the priest as a condition of absolution. In the Catholic Bible, Douay version, it is said (Matt. iv. 17; Luke xxiv. 47), "Do penance, for the kingdom of God is at hand;" "That penance and remission of sins should be preached in his name." * So also, in Acts ii. 38, Peter says, "Do penance." The penances enjoined as conditions of absolution are chiefly alms-giving, fasting, and prayer.

Indulgences mean (1) the substitution of something

---

* The Holy Bible, translated from the Latin Vulgate; the Old Testament first published by the English College at Douay, A.D. 1609; and the New Testament first published by the English College at Rheims, A.D. 1582.

else in the place of penance; and (2) the removal of temporal punishments in this life or the next. For, according to the Roman-Catholic doctrine, all sins incur a double penalty, eternal and temporal. Eternal punishment is separation from God, and loss of the beatific vision. This is removed by the atonement of Christ; and his atonement is received by penitence and faith, through baptism. But the temporal consequences of sin remain, and are to be endured in this world, and the other. Temporal punishment in the other world is purgatory. The church claims the power of remitting this by indulgences. But, down to the time of St. Thomas, opinions differed in the church as to their value. Much opposition existed against selling indulgences for money; but this was too profitable to be given up. Sextus VI., in 1477, first applied indulgences to the relief of souls in purgatory; before him, it had been confined to church punishments in the present life.* Much objection was made to this doctrine by Catholic theologians. One argument being, that if the pope possessed this power, he ought at once to relieve all souls from purgatory. At present, however, indulgences are given on various grounds. In 1860, the present pope offered an indulgence of one hundred years to every one who would fight against Victor Emanuel. In some Italian

* Hase, Handbuch der Protestantischen Polemik. Gieseler, 2; cccxxv.

churches you see the notice: "Every mass performed in this church delivers a soul from purgatory." In the church of S. Pudienza at Rome, it is declared, "Every person visiting this church obtains for every day an indulgence of three thousand years." In the church of S. Lorenzo before the Walls, "Forgiveness of all sins" is offered to every one worshipping therein. It is one of the impenetrable mysteries of Roman-Catholic belief, that a man should take the trouble of going to one church for the pitiful indulgence of three thousand years, when by visiting another he can obtain remission for all his sins. Perrone, the modern Roman-Catholic controversialist, exultingly declares that scarcely any one can be found so destitute of the means of grace as not to be able to obtain an indulgence somehow.

The sacraments of the church are indeed admirably adapted to all parts of human life. The infant enters the kingdom of heaven by baptism. The youth receives new grace by confirmation. The sacrament of penance removes the effect of mortal sins, and places one again in a state of grace. The sacrament of orders gives the priest the power of applying the other sacraments. The sacrament of the eucharist, or mass, brings God visibly before the eyes of the congregation. In it the God-Man is sacrificed anew, day by day, for human sin. The faithful who partake of it, receive new life in their souls, by feeding on the body and blood of Christ. Matrimony is elevated to a sacrament, and made indissoluble. Its essence, however, consists, according to the Roman Catholics, in the consent of the two parties, and the presence of a priest. If, therefore, two young people, to whose marriage the parents refuse their consent, and whom the priest refuses to marry, lie in wait for him in his walk, and spring out from the trees and say, "We take each other in marriage," this is a legitimate union.

No Catholic marriage can be dissolved; but the church may declare that if certain impediments existed, it never really was a marriage, which comes to very much the same thing. Fifteen such impediments are mentioned by Romish theologians; such as a mistake as to the person intended, a vow of celibacy, affinity, compulsion, difference of worship.

Extreme unction is founded on the saying of James, "If any among you be sick, call the elders of the church, and let them pray over him, anointing him with oil in the name of Christ; and the prayer of faith shall save the sick, and the Lord shall raise him up." But this can hardly apply to the Roman-Catholic sacrament of extreme unction, which is only given to dying persons, and with no expectation of curing them.

The doctrine of transubstantiation teaches that in the Lord's Supper, when the priest utters the words, "This is my body, and this is my blood," the bread and wine are changed, as to their substance, into the body and blood, soul and spirit, of Christ; while their accidents remain the same as before. This doctrine is based on the philosophy of Aristotle, in which every thing is either substance or accident. Accidents are all that can be perceived by the senses, as color, shape, weight, perfume, flavor, &c., — in short, all outward phenomena. Substance is that which stands under them, and supports them; that in which these qualities inhere.

By means of this doctrine, a mysterious influence is no doubt conveyed to the believers, which touches the imagination, and produces awe.

But the evil is, that, like other sacraments, it becomes a charm. Over some altars it is written, "Every mass performed at this altar delivers a soul from purgatory." The mass works its effect whether any are present to receive an influence or not; consequently masses are often offered when no one is present, or only a few.

No doubt good is done by the sacraments. A good priest puts his soul and heart into them, and so they become full of soul and heart. There is also something touching and tender in the thought of the church walking with its children through life, reaching its hand to them all the way; taking the infant, and baptizing it into the kingdom of heaven; calling together the young, and in their white confirmation robes leading them up to become the servants of Christ; relieving the sense of sin by hearing its confession, and absolving the penitent; bringing down God into the church day by day in the awful mystery of the tremendous eucharist; making a sacred body apart from the world, in its priesthood, standing separate from life, outside of the world, to move it, not to be moved by it; sanctifying the joy of marriage with a holier bliss; and touching the brow of the dying with a passport into eternal rest. As an ideal, it is all very graceful and pleasant. But is it true? Does it on the whole do good? These are the questions ultimately to be asked of all human institutions.

Is this sacramental system true Christianity? Did Jesus teach any such system? Is there any thing like it in the New Testament? Where, in the four Gospels, do we find the priesthood, the system of confession and absolution, the doctrine of grace given through external acts and ceremonies? Is not this a revival of that temple worship and those ritual observances which Jesus himself opposed most strongly? Would any one, in reading the four Gospels, imagine that Christ ever meant to establish such a ritual system as this? This is the real difficulty with Romanism. It is not by a few texts, taken here and there, that we can decide the point; but by seeing if the general teaching of Jesus inculcated that by belonging to a church and partaking of its sacraments men were to be saved. On the contrary, he taught continually, that we are saved by our faith in God, our love to man, our fidelity in duty, our willingness to follow him in his piety and humanity. The sermon on the mount and the parables have not a word about sacraments in them. All there is faith, hope, love, and obedience.

The Protestant Church, following the Apostle Paul, says we are justified by faith, and not by ceremonial or sacramental works. Christianity does not consist in assisting at the mass, or in confessing to the priest, but in trusting in God and his love; in having faith in that divine pity which came to us eminently in Christ. It is a state of the heart, not the performance of ceremonies. To be justified by faith does not mean that we are saved by believing this or that opinion; but that we are saved by confidence in God's love, and by having a childlike reliance on his fatherly goodness. If you wish to have your son safe amid the temptations of life, teach him to confide in you; make him understand that he can always come to you in his difficulties; that he can find no better friend than his father and mother. As long as you retain his confidence, he is safe. As long as he tells you every thing, he is in no danger. And so God wishes us to tell him every thing, to bring all our troubles to him, and feel that he is the best friend we have. M. Renan, in his Life of Paul, says of the doctrine of justification by faith:

"This doctrine of Paul, opposed apparently to common sense, has been really salutary and conducive to human freedom. It has separated Christianity from Judaism, and Protestantism from Catholicism. There is a twofold evil in the belief that the performance of religious actions procures forgiveness and salvation. First, it destroys morality by persuading the devotee that he can enter heaven in spite of God. The most hard-hearted Jews, and the most selfish and cruel usurers, have imagined that by carefully keeping the ceremonial law they would compel God to save them. The Catholic, in the time of Louis XI., fancied he could defend himself against the Almighty as by the technicalities of a legal process; and that, assisted by a sufficient number of masses, any scoundrel most odious to the Deity could, according to the most regular methods, enter heaven, and force God to receive him into his society. To this impiety, to which Judaism had been brought by Talmudism, and to which Christianity has been brought by Mediæval Catholicism, Paul has applied the most vigorous remedy, declaring that man is not justified by any works of the law, but by the faith of Jesus Christ. This is why this doctrine, apparently so illiberal, has been the text of all reformers, the lever by which Wickliff, Huss, Luther, Calvin, and St. Cyran have resisted the old traditions of routine, of idle trust in a priest, and in a kind of external goodness, quite independent of any change of heart.

"The other objection to these outside observances is that they create incessant scruples. Being considered to have a value in themselves, *ex opere operato*, apart from the state of mind of him who performs them, they open the way to all the subtilties of a minute casuistry. The legal work becomes a receipt, the success of which depends on its precise and exact performance. In this point, also, the Talmud and Catholicism have come upon common ground."

The essential doctrinal antagonism of Romanism and Protestantism has its root in the answer to this question: "Are we saved by faith or by sacraments?" The other doctrines of theology, such as the deity of Christ, the trinity, total depravity, the atonement, are not peculiar to Romanism or Protestantism, but were inherited by both, from the church of the Middle Ages. The early Greek Church invented the doctrine of the trinity. The Latin Church afterward developed that of total depravity and the atonement.

But there is no doubt, if we are to take Christianity from the teaching of Jesus and Paul, that the doctrine of salvation by sacraments is false. It is not by ceremonies any more than by creeds that the soul of man is made true and pure. And yet let us admit the good that has been done by pious and devoted men who have believed in this sacramental salvation. It has been daily bread for the souls of thousands in every age; it has tended to open a way for the teachings of Jesus to enter the mind and heart. "Every priest," says the Epistle to the Hebrews, "standeth daily ministering, and offering oftentimes the same sacrifices which can never take away sins;" nevertheless, he may often make men better and happier by his labors.

In one of the chambers of the Vatican there hang opposite to each other two pictures, which are considered by many to be the two finest paintings from the hand of man. One is the Communion of St. Jerome, by Domenichino. The saint, old, decrepit, at the point of death, is receiving the sacramental wafer, with an expression of rapture on his face, — a rapture of reverence, gratitude, and love. This is the apotheosis of sacramental religion. On the opposite wall is the Transfiguration of Jesus, by Rafaelle. Jesus, with Moses and Elijah on either hand, floats in the air, lifted above earth by the power of this great communion of mind and heart. The faith in things unseen, which can remove mountains, had removed the veil between time and eternity, and brought the three great prophets face to face. This is the religion of the spirit, — not of form, nor of the letter, but of faith, hope, and love!

It is far higher than the other. The covenant of works comes to an end. Ceremonies will cease. Penances will be abolished. The outward sacraments of water, bread, and wine will at last be no longer needed. But the religion of faith, hope, and love, uniting us to God, and to man, will always remain. These three abide for ever. This is what transfigures time, and this is what opens the way into eternity.

CHAPTER III.

Priesthood and Ritual of the Roman-Catholic Church.

ACCORDING to the Roman-Catholic doctrine, the clergy is a body instituted by Christ, and inheriting special grace from him, in an unbroken line of descent. It alone possesses the power of the sacraments and the government of the church. Through the medium of the clergy alone does Christ communicate with the people. They alone have the power of opening or closing the gates of heaven. This hierarchy, which consists of bishops, priests, and deacons, is instituted by God.* The special work of a priest is to offer sacrifice. The eucharist is the sacrifice in the New Testament corresponding to the Jewish sacrifices in the Old Testament. The Roman-Catholic priest therefore is the fulfilment, on a higher plane, of the Jewish priesthood.

---

* "Si quis dixerit in Ecclesiâ Catholica non esse hierarchiam divina ordinatione institutam, quæ constat ex episcopis, presbyteris, et ministris, anathema sit." (Synod of Trent, Sess. xxiii. canon 6.)

The Protestant Church does not consider its clergy as priests, but as ministers of the word. Their work is not to offer sacrifice, but to preach the gospel. They are successors, not of the Jewish priest, but of the Jewish prophet. This is the radical distinction between the clergy in the two churches. The one stands at an altar; the other, in a pulpit. One receives his authority from the priesthood by ordination; the other, from the people by election. The Protestant minister is one of the people: he is no more a priest than the rest. He is on a level with his brethren. But the Roman-Catholic idea was expressed by Lainez, General of the Jesuits, in his famous speech at the Council of Trent. He declared that the people were like sheep, and the priest was their shepherd. "Sheep," said he, "are beasts without reason; and therefore ought not to take any part in the government of the church. That belongs to the priesthood alone." *

But though Catholics have sometimes said, in an extravagant way, that the worst priest was better than the most pious layman, yet this idea has never been thoroughly carried out in the church. One of the sacraments, that of marriage, is performed not by the priest, but by the parties themselves, in the priest's presence. For the Roman Catholics have the true idea of marriage, as consisting essentially in the consent of the man and woman. Most of the sacraments, in

* Sarpi, — quoted by Hase, p. 110.

cases of necessity, can be administered by laymen. Laymen can baptize, and their baptism is valid. In the Middle Ages, knights confessed each other, and gave absolution to their dying comrades. Monasticism itself is a kind of included Protestantism. For why do men and women go into convents to save their souls by penance and prayer, if they are satisfied with the salvation which comes from sacraments? They go to find a higher religion than the priest can give, in direct communion with God himself.

One objection to the Roman-Catholic idea of the priesthood is, that it is opposed to Christian equality and Christian brotherhood. It introduces into the church a caste, like that of the Brahmins in India. Christians are not all brethren in this system; but the laity are brethren, and the priests are fathers. Consequently a Roman-Catholic priest is usually called father; though Jesus has said, "Call no man father on earth, for one is your Father in heaven, and all ye are brethren." Accordingly Martin Luther declared that all Christians were priests, and that there was no real distinction between clergy and laity. "Whoever has received Christian baptism," said he, "is priest, bishop, and pope. Two or three laymen, meeting together in the name of Christ, make a church; they can baptize, administer the sacrament, preach, and absolve each other's sins."

This was certainly the original idea in Christianity. God was to "pour out his Spirit on all flesh;" "On my servants, and on my hand-maidens, I will pour out of my Spirit, saith the Lord, and they shall prophesy;" "I will write the law in their hearts, and ye shall no more need to teach each other, saying, Know the Lord, for all shall know me, from the least of you to the greatest of you;" "The anointing [or christening] which you have received remains in you, and ye do not need that any shall teach you."* Peter, the head of the Catholic Church, called all Christians "a holy nation, a peculiar priesthood."† Irenæus wrote, "All the good belong to the priesthood."‡ Tertullian said, "Are not all the laity priests? Where three of them meet in Christ's name, there is a church."§ Consistent and logical Protestants therefore ought to admit that the laity, both men and women, have full power to preach and pray in public, and to administer the sacraments of baptism, and the Lord's Supper. If some men are set apart for this, it is for convenience, and on the principle of division of labor. In the Congregational Church this principle of equality is more fully asserted than in any other except by the "Friends." In the Cambridge platform, it is said that there may be a church where there is no minister, and that a man ceases to be a clergyman when he ceases to be the minister of a church; that he becomes a layman the moment that he loses his office as pastor

---

* 1 John ii. 27.
† 1 Peter ii. 9.
‡ iv. 20
§ Exhort. Cast. c. 7.

of a church; and becomes a clergyman again, when he is elected pastor of another church. This is the true Protestant idea, thoroughly carried out.

According to the rule of the Roman Church, the priest must be unmarried. To become a priest is to take a vow of celibacy for life. This, however, is not a matter of faith, but of discipline; and the Roman-Catholic Church might, at any time, allow its priests to marry. This is a reform loudly demanded by many in the church itself, and will, probably, be the first step taken in a new church reformation. If the Ecumenical Council, by its decrees, puts the church in opposition to the temporal governments of Europe, and also in opposition to modern science and all free thought, the result may be that one or more Catholic nations will separate from its communion, and become national churches. They will probably not become Protestants, but will retain the Catholic ritual and ceremonies. But, in such a case, they will immediately allow the priests to marry, as in the Greek Church. For though Paul thought it more convenient not to marry, and praised celibacy, yet, in the Epistle to Timothy, he called "forbidding to marry" a "doctrine of devils," and told Titus that a bishop ought to be the husband of one wife. And there is something almost pathetic in the fact that the Apostle Peter, the head of that church which has made celibacy the law of its priesthood, should have had *a mother-in-law*, and should have been said by

Paul to carry his wife about with him on his missionary journeys. One would not like to hurt the feelings of a good Roman Catholic by reading the text about Peter's wife's mother being sick of a fever.

The arguments in favor of an unmarried priesthood are, that they can give their whole time to the ministry, not having to care for wife and children; that they are more ready to encounter dangers, and go on missions; they are not made anxious by dread of poverty; and they are more reverenced by having no bride but the church, no children but their parishioners. All these may be very good reasons why young clergymen should not be immediately married, and why some should not marry at all. But it is no reason for forbidding all to marry by an inflexible law. Riding by the shore of the Mediterranean, I once invited into the carriage a priest, whom we overtook walking, and we discussed this question together in very bad French. He said, "How can you Protestant ministers attend to your duties, and visit your parishioners, when your wife or children are sick, and you have to stay at home and nurse them?" To which I replied, that not having the experience of a married man, and living a solitary life, he could not enter into the feelings of his parishioners, but was placed apart from them. "A good wife," said I, "makes a man stronger to do all his duties, and puts twice as much judgment and force into him for his work. It is not good for the man to be alone.

He may have less care and more time when he is not married; but he has not so much heart, nor so much power for his work."

All the Roman clergy are divided into two classes, — regulars and seculars. The secular clergy are the bishops and parish priests. The regulars are the members of monastic institutions, — monks and friars. All the orders of monks take the three vows of poverty, chastity, and obedience.

There seems to be something natural to man in this monastic system. It is found in all religions. The Jews had their monks in the Essenes and Therapeutæ: the Mohammedans, Brahmins, and Buddhists have their anchorites, living either alone or in cloisters; and here, in America, we have our Protestant monks and nuns in the Shakers. The Buddhist monks live in great monasteries, and take the same three vows as the Roman Catholics. They are all mendicants, going out every day to get their food. They pray with a rosary, counting their beads, like the Catholics.

It is no doubt true that the cloister has brought consolation and peace to many a poor soul, who has not strength for the battle of life. The community principle, in the cloister-life, is a good one. It is to be wished that we had Protestant communities, to which lonely and weary men and women could go, and find friendship and relief from perpetual anxiety. The struggle of life is so fierce among us, competition is so active, that thousands find it hard to live, even by working all the time. Now if there were Christian communities well arranged, where by the economies of combined households, and by thorough organization, they could have comfort and rest for a fair day's work, it would no doubt be a blessing. Such communities as the Shakers, and that of Rapp, show that this is perfectly feasible. They all have a pecuniary success. And so it was with the monasteries of the Catholic Church. They gradually absorbed into themselves a large part of the wealth of many countries, and were suppressed for this reason, and their property confiscated by the governments of Catholic nations. In the Middle Ages, they did great good. They were the refuge of the oppressed, the last retreat of learning; they became teachers of youth, and the civilizers of the community. But they were very apt to run the course of other institutions. At first, founded by good men for good purposes, they were useful and pure. Their virtues gave them influence, power, and wealth. Then power and wealth corrupted them, and they became indolent, luxurious, vicious. Then they grew odious, and were abolished; and others, better and purer, took their place.

No one can be present at a function of the Roman-Catholic Church on a great festival, and in a magnificent cathedral, without feeling the impressive nature of the ceremony. The grand architecture and the splendid music; the processions of priests in their gorgeous robes and vestments; the mysterious ceremonies at the high altar, genuflexions, the smoke of incense, swinging of censers, elevation of the host, ringing of bells,—all is calculated to touch the imagination, like a solemn tragedy. There is something essentially dramatic in the whole ritual, and most people love the drama. The worship of the Virgin in the Catholic Church also touches a cord in the human heart. When God is represented as clothed in terror, an awful monarch; when Christ is revered as the Judge whose chief attribute is justice: then comes the Virgin Mary, combining all the sweetest traits of tender womanhood. She has the purity of the girl, and the devoted kind ness of the mother. She is the friend of the sinners; she takes them all as she finds them; she never chides, finds fault, or condemns; her only work is to save. And then she has such power in heaven, as the Mother of God, that she *can* save us. All who put themselves under her protection are safe. Mary, in the Catholic Church, is a creation of the human heart, which had been defrauded of its heavenly Father by fierce and terrific doctrines. They took away the love of God, they took away the blessed grace of Jesus; and so the poor empty heart turned to Mary, put her in heaven, and then took her for its God, its Christ, its Saviour. It can come nearer to her than to the Trinity: she is more human. All sweet and great names therefore are given to her in the prayers of the Catholic. She is "Mother of God," "Star of the Sea," "Spouse of the Holy Ghost," "Door of Heaven," "Queen of the Angels," "Rose among thorns," "Ocean of love." And yet I sometimes wonder what the real Mary in heaven thinks of all this; and how her modesty must be pained by this great wave of worship, coming up to her from earth every day, — she who was only a sweet, pure woman. It seems too hard that she should have to hear it all, and be made unhappy by being thus an object of worship which so often takes the heart of the devotee from God, and from Christ. Think how very sadly any good woman would feel at finding herself in heaven made the object of worship. I think Mary is really much to be pitied.

Jesus has told us not to use "vain repetitions in our prayers as the heathen do, who think they shall be heard for their much speaking," and gives us his own prayer as an example of what is short but comprehensive. And then the Catholic makes a rosary, in which he repeats the Ave Maria one hundred and fifty times, and the Lord's Prayer ten times. The Catholic prayer-book tells us that this rosary "was composed in heaven, dictated by the Holy Ghost, and delivered to the faithful by the Angel Gabriel, Saint Elizabeth, and the Church of Christ." * The same book, published by authority of the bishops of the church, has litanies to many different saints, as Saint Joseph, Saint Teresa, Saint Bernard, Saint Philomena, and — what seems very curious, — one "To the

---

* Saint Vincent's Manual, p. 428.

Infant Jesus," and another to the "Blessed Sacrament." Do the Catholics believe that there is an infant Jesus now in heaven? Is Christ an infant now? And if not, how can they pray to a being who does not exist? This litany addresses the infant Jesus eighty-nine times. It says, for example, "Infant, crying in the crib, have mercy on us;" "Infant, equal to thy Father;" "Infant, subject to thy mother;" "Infant, in want of food;" "Infant, dwelling in heaven," &c., "have mercy on us." All these eighty-nine prayers are addressed to an infant who does not exist; for certainly Christ is not an infant now.

The litany of the blessed sacrament has a great number of petitions addressed to the eucharist, asking it to have mercy. It says, "O wheat of the elect;" "O wine which makest virgins;" "O supersubstantial bread," "Chalice of benediction," "Heavenly antidote," &c., "have mercy on us." It is true that, according to the doctrine of the Roman Church, the bread and wine are changed, as to their substance, into the body and blood of Christ. It is true that he means to worship, not the bread and wine, but the God manifested by them. But what the worshipper adores, in this prayer, is not this substance which is invisible, but the accidents, the outward phenomena, which are not changed. When he says, "O wheat! O wine! O bread! O chalice!" he is adoring the visible form under which God is supposed to be present. And just so the Athenian, who worshipped the statue of the Phidian Jupiter, intended to worship not the marble, but the God manifested by the statue. He did not mean to worship stone and gold and ivory. If the one was idolatry, the other is idolatry. So when the Catholic adores the crucifix, or pictures, he means to have his mind ascend through these to God. But that is just what an intelligent Hindoo will tell you about his images of Vischnu and Siva. The danger is that the ignorant and unspiritual will, in both cases, make a fetich of the idol, the picture, the cross, the wafer, and worship the visible part, letting his devotion stop there.

The church of Rome has often committed the fault of letting itself down to the level of the ignorant worshipper, instead of lifting him up to hers. The motive was good, the spirit amiable. She wished, like Paul, to become all things to all men, in order to save them. Only she carried it too far; and instead of raising them, she was sometimes drawn down herself. To meet the tastes and wishes of the Pagans, the early church allowed a great deal of Paganism to enter into Christianity. The Pagans worshipped deified men, and each had his favorite saint to whom he prayed. The Roman sailors worshipped Venus, and called her "Star of the sea," and "Queen of heaven." The Pagans had sacred images, fallen from heaven. So have the Catholics. The Pagans adorned their images with flowers, knelt to them, offered incense to them, carried them in processions, and made pilgrimages to them. So do the Catholics. The Pagans had statues which winked and nodded. So have the Catholics. The statues at Athens sweated before the battle of Cheronea. The statue of Mars, at Rome, sweated during Tully's consulship. Antony's statue, on the Alban Mount, bled before the fight at Actium. The ancient Romans kissed the toe of the Pontifex Maximus, and the ancient Druids kissed the toe of their chief priest. Holy water is a Pagan institution. It stood in the same part of the temples as in the churches, and was used to touch the body. They called it lustral water. Incense is Pagan. Roman Catholics celebrate the Purification of the Virgin on the 2d of February: the old Romans celebrated the miraculous conception of Jove on the 2d of February. The priest's vestments come from the old Roman priests, and have the same names.

The Roman-Catholic churches are full of the relics of saints. A church in Cologne has, built into its walls, the bones of 11,000 martyred virgins. In the cathedral of Cologne are shown the skulls of the three wise men who came to see the infant Jesus. It is said there is extant, in different places, enough of the wood of the true cross to make a dozen of the same size as the original one. The holy shirt of Jesus is kept in the Lateran Church at Rome, and also in the church of Argenteuil, and a third is kept at Treves. In the Middle Ages they exhibited to the people a feather from the wing of the Archangel Michael;

one of the bones of Moses; one of the thorns from the flesh of the Apostle Paul; some of the tears of the Redeemer at the grave of Lazarus; and a member of Parliament in England lately stated in his place that in eight Catholic churches to-day there are flasks in which is kept the milk from the bosom of the Holy Virgin. But all this is of pagan origin. There are immense buildings in India called Topes, erected before the birth of Christ by the Buddhists, over the relics of their saint. One in Ceylon contains his tooth. Another covers the place where his shadow once fell. Pausanias says that in the Greek temples they preserved an egg believed to have been laid by Leda, and some of the clay out of which Prometheus had formed men. In a mosque near Mecca is kept the leg of mutton which Mohammed was about to eat, but which spoke to him and said, "Eat me not, I am poisoned."

In many Roman-Catholic churches are to be seen votive offerings presented by those who have been cured from disease or saved from danger by the Virgin, or by some saint. The walls are often entirely covered with arms, legs, and hands made of marble, or silver, hung up by those who have been cured of diseases in those organs. But in the museums of Europe you find exactly similar images and votive offerings, from Roman, Greek, or Egyptian tombs. These same images were suspended in the pagan temples, for the same reason; and the custom is often alluded to by classic writers. Certainly there is no harm in borrowing a custom from the ancients, if it is a good one. I do not blame the Roman-Catholic Church for being willing to take good things wherever it can find them. The reverence for relics is natural to man. Who would not be thankful to obtain a piece of the original manuscript of one of Paul's Epistles to put into his collection of autographs? Pilgrimages to the graves of saints are natural. We go to Mount Vernon to see the tomb of Washington; and Mr. Everett gave a lecture one hundred and fifty times in order to raise money to buy the Mount Vernon estate for the nation. But to allow false relics to be manufactured is not the part of a true church. Thousands of pilgrims every year go on their knees up the Scala Santa or Holy Stairs at Rome, supposed to have been brought by the Empress Helena from Jerusalem in 326, and believed to be the steps of the house of Pilate. There is not the least historic evidence, or probability, that when Jerusalem was destroyed, these steps were preserved or could have been. Yet the papal bulls give nine years' indulgence for each of the twenty-eight steps so ascended by a pilgrim.

"God is a spirit," said Jesus, "and those who worship him must worship him in spirit and in truth." Devotion is not enough to make Christian worship: there should also be truth. The Roman-Catholic Church has an infinite good nature: it has taken pains to suit its worship to the passions, prejudices, and habits of mankind. Therefore its churches are crowded, and its people are more devout than Protestants. They worship *more*. But is their worship purifying and elevating? The Catholics worship more than the Protestants. But the Mohammedans worship more than the Catholics. The Hindoos worship more than the Mohammedans. Is it the *quantity* or the *quality* of prayer which makes it acceptable to God? Two commands Jesus gave in relation to prayer, which seem to have been forgotten by his disciples. One was, Do not pray *much*, as though that would help you. Do not make *long* prayers, or use many repetitions, for God knows already what you want, and says, "Before they call I will answer, and while they are yet speaking I will hear." The other command was, Do not pray in public, to be seen of men; but go into your closet to pray. The chief part of the public worship of the Catholic Church is in order to be seen. It is an exhibition. When the priest performs mass he does not speak to the congregation, nor with them, but in Latin; and he cannot be heard, for he turns his back to the people. They follow him in their prayer-books as well as they can, and look at the elevation of the host when the bell rings. In Protestant churches there is an attempt at least to have all pray together, minister and people.

However, we do not mean to say that Protestant worship is what it ought to be, any more than the Catholic worship. Each has faults of its own, and opposite faults. One has in it more of love than of truth: the other more of truth than of love. That is the distinction of the two churches all through. One is cold, but pure; the other is warm, but turbid with very mixed sentiments. Protestantism has more morality and less piety; Catholicism, more piety and less morality. Romanism is more loving, gentle, friendly; Protestantism is more truthful, pure, and conscientious. All this goes into the worship. The Roman Catholics put every thing into their worship, true or false, which seems to do good to the worshipper, or to make him happy. Protestants are so careful to have only what is true, that their worship becomes an occupation for the intellect, and grows cold.

One day, perhaps, we shall have a service which will unite the merits of both; a ritual which shall combine fine architecture, music, and paintings, with simplicity, purity, and Christian truth. Our churches, standing always open, will be the religious homes of the people, into which they can always turn, and rest their souls from the weariness of daily tasks. They will not be merely for prayer, but also for all humane action, work, culture, and social intercourse.

In Catholic countries the poorest man or woman, living in misery at home, has a share in the noblest and most beautiful building in the city. Every morning they have as good a right to go into their magnificent church, as the nobility or the king. There is fine music; there is a daily mass; there are pictures, the masterpieces of art; there are statues and exquisite carvings in marble and wood. There is something for eye, ear, and heart, as well as for the intellect. Cannot we do the same? Why should not the walls of our churches be hung with illustrations of the life of Jesus, great Protestant paintings? Why should there not be every day, at suitable hours, the finest devotional music? Why should we not have lighted, warmed, and handsomely furnished parlors, opened every evening for conversation? Where the Catholics have done well, let us not be afraid to imitate them; and, if we can, to better their example.

CHAPTER IV.

RESULTS OF THIS DISCUSSION.

THERE are two different views of the Christian Church: the one places the essence of it in its visible part, the other in its invisible part.

The first of these may be called the Church of the Mustard Seed; the second, the Church of the Leaven. The one is an outward, visible tree, in which the birds come and build their nests. The second is the little leaven, hid in three measures of meal, gradually leavening the whole.

The true Christian Church comprehends both ideas. It is an inward communion, and an outward organization. Roman Catholics also believe in the inward spirit of communion in the church, as its soul. Protestants also believe in an outward organization of the church, as its body. Every living thing has a soul and a body: without soul, the body is only a corpse; without body, the soul is only a ghost.

Both Roman Catholics and Protestants believe in the church visible and the church invisible. But the one makes the visible church the root, and the invisible church the fruit; the other makes the invisible church the root, and the visible church the fruit.

The Roman Catholic teaches that safety consists in being in outward, open communion with the true, visible church, of which the pope is the head. As long as you are in that, you are safe. Protestants teach that safety consists in being in inward spiritual communion with the invisible church of truth and love, of which the invisible Christ is the head.

The question resolves itself into this: What are we to do first? What is the first step to take? The Roman Catholic says the first thing to be done is to have faith in the visible church, and to submit to its authority; till this is done, nothing is done; when this is done, all things else will follow. The Protestant says the first thing is to be united to the invisible church by faith in Christ, and obedience to him; when this is done, all is done.

The essential religion of the Roman-Catholic Church is in the sacrament. A sacrament is an outward act, which, when duly performed, conveys an inward power. The absolute importance of being in communion with the visible church lies in this, — that otherwise you cannot have access to the sacraments, which are essential to the life of the soul.

Any Protestants, therefore, whether Baptists, High-Church Episcopalians, or others, who make any external ordinances essential to salvation, are really planted on the Roman-Catholic idea of the church, and not on the Protestant idea. The great growth of the Baptist body in America is because they make of baptism a sacrament; implying that no one is safe until he is baptized. If you wish to increase the visible church, you can easily do so, by making it essential to salvation to belong to it.

The Roman-Catholic principle, as distinguished from the Protestant, is this: "Do good, and you will be good." The Protestant principle is: "Be good, and you will do good."

The Catholic begins on the circumference and works in to the centre; the Protestant begins at the centre and works out to the circumference.

There is evidently truth in both principles. An outward action, good or bad, reacts on the soul. An inward conviction, intention, affection, works its way out into the conduct. Consequently, it will not do to condemn wholly the Roman-Catholic principle. The real objection is not that it is false, but that it becomes false by being stated exclusively. If you say, "A man may be made better by joining a church, and receiving its sacraments," you say what is true. If you say, "He can be made better only by joining the church, and receiving its sacraments," you say what is false.

Materialism says, "We are made what we are by outward circumstances, and outward influences." Spiritualism says, "We are made what we are by an inward formative principle." One teaches that the body makes the soul; the other, that the soul makes the body. Materialism is at one with the Roman-Catholic theory; Protestantism with the transcendental theory.

To show how entirely the principle of the Roman-Catholic Church is to work from without, I quote the commandments of the church from St. Vincent's Manual (page 25).

"COMMANDMENTS OF THE CHURCH.

"1. The Catholic Church commands her children, on Sundays and holy days of obligation, to be present at the holy sacrifice of the mass, to rest from servile work on those days, and to keep them holy.

"2. She commands them to abstain from flesh on all days of fasting and abstinence; and on fast days to eat but one meal.

"3. She commands them to confess their sins to their pastor, at least once a year.

"4. She commands them to receive the blessed sacrament at least once a year, and that at Easter, or during the paschal time.

"5. To contribute to the support of our pastors.

"6. Not to marry within the fourth degree of kindred, nor privately without witnesses, nor to solemnize marriage at certain prohibited times."

The condemnation of the Roman-Catholic Church is in the extravagance of its pretensions. If it demanded less, it would receive more. It declares itself the one infallible, apostolic, holy church, out of which is no salvation. By this extravagance it incurs the Master's sentence: "Whoso exalteth himself shall be abased." For this arrogant assumption implies that there are no Christians outside the Church of Rome: consequently no Christian goodness. Therefore every good man and woman in Protestant Churches is a refutation of the Roman-Catholic claim.

The assumption of Rome is not that it produces a better sort of Christianity than is created by Protestantism, but that its own kind is the only kind. It ought to follow that all the goodness of Christendom is contained in Roman-Catholic countries. These should be full of holiness, truth, purity, conscientiousness, and love. The difference should be so evident as to need no argument. But it is not so. The morals of Protestant nations are at least as good as those of Catholic nations. Hence the Catholic assumption is untenable, and the Catholic claim is false.

Protestantism has been long enough in the world to enable us to judge of this. Jesus teaches us that the tree is known by its fruits. He declares that a good tree cannot bring forth evil fruit, nor a corrupt tree good fruit. "By their fruits ye shall know them." Let us apply this test to the Roman-Catholic and Protestant Churches.

A legitimate fruit of the Roman-Catholic tree is persecution on account of opinion. The Roman Church assumes to know certainly what doctrines are true and what false. But false doctrines, it says, if believed, will destroy the soul for ever. If by burning a few hundred or a few thousand individuals, it can save whole nations from becoming heretics, it saves hundred of millions from eternal fire. Accordingly, it holds itself justified in so doing. Hence, by a natural consequence, come the Inquisition, Torquemada, Alva, the Bartholomew Massacre.

The present pope, in his "Encyclical Letter" and "Syllabus," declares this doctrine very plainly. In the "Encyclical," he says there are those "who dare to teach . . against the doctrine of the holy Scriptures, of the church, and of the holy Fathers, that condition of society the best, in which the civil power does not recognize the obligation to coerce by enacted penalties the violation of the Catholic religion, except so far as the public peace may require it." He also calls it remarkably impudent to affirm "that the church has no right to coerce the violators of her laws by temporal punishments." In the twenty-fourth section of the "Syllabus," he also condemns the opinion that "the church has no power to employ force, nor has she any temporal power, direct or indirect." It may be said that Catholics generally do not share this view. But we can scarcely open any Catholic journal without finding some declaration in this spirit. Thus the "Univers," the ultramontane journal, published in France, speaks thus: —

"A heretic, examined and convicted by the church, used to be delivered over to the secular power, and punished with death. Nothing has ever appeared to us more natural, or more necessary. More than one hundred thousand persons perished in consequence of the heresy of Wickliff; a still greater number by that of John Huss. It would not be possible to calculate the bloodshed caused by the heresy of Luther, and it is not yet over. After three centuries we are at the eve of a recommencement. The prompt repression of the disciples of Luther, and a crusade against Protestantism, would have spared Europe three centuries of discord and of catastrophes, in which France and civilization may perish. It was under the influence of such reflections that I wrote the phrase which has so excited the virtuous indignation of the red journals. Here it is: 'For my part, I avow frankly my regret is not only that they did not sooner burn John Huss, but that they did not equally burn Luther; and I regret, further, that there had not been at the same time some prince sufficiently pious and politic to have made a crusade against the Protestants.'"

If it be thought that such doctrines cannot be held by Catholics in America, we refer to the following passage extracted from Mr. Orestes A. Brownson's "Review," to show the contrary. Mr. Brownson is an American, educated a Protestant, for many years the advocate of the broadest religious liberty. If such a man as this, on becoming a Catholic, defends persecution, it is evident that nothing in modern civilization, or modern education, can neutralize the logic which carries every consistent Catholic to that conclusion. Thus spoke Mr. Brownson, some years ago indeed; but he has never retracted his declaration.

"The church is a kingdom and a power, and as such must have a supreme chief; and his authority is to be exercised over states as well as individuals. If the pope directed the Roman Catholics of this country to overthrow the constitution, sell its territory, and annex it as a dependent province to the dominions of Napoleon, they would be bound to obey. It is the intention of the pope to possess this country."

In another Romish periodical, a writer signing himself "Apostolicus," thus confirms the bold statement of the more illustrious writer: —

"I say, with Brownson, that if the church should declare that the constitution and the very existence of this or any other country should be extinguished, it is a solemn ordinance of God himself; and every good Catholic would be bound, under the terrible penalty pronounced against the disobedient, to obey."

The "Freeman's Journal," the organ of the Archbishop of New York, also says, —

"The pope of Rome has supreme authority over every square foot of surface on this globe. His rights are circumscribed only by the ends of the earth, and the consummation of the ages."

Persecution for opinion's sake is therefore one of the fruits native to this Roman-Catholic tree. Whenever and wherever it does not bear this fruit it is because it is feeble, and grows in an uncongenial soil. Give it strength enough, and this fruit will immediately reappear. But usually it has not been wanting. Witness the crusade preached against the Albigenses, in the thirteenth century, by order of Innocent III., in which Arnold, the papal legate, triumphantly declared that he had put to the sword, in one city, twenty thousand persons, sparing neither rank, sex, nor age. Witness the thirty-one thousand nine hundred and twelve persons burnt alive in Spain alone, by the holy Inquisition, between 1633 and 1808. Witness the Bartholomew Massacre in France, to commemorate which, medals were struck in Rome by order of the Pope. Witness the horrible cruelties of Alva in the Netherlands, by order of Philip II., who only lived to obey the Church of Rome, and do as his confessor ordered him.

Is the church which has ordered and permitted these cruelties and atrocities the only holy and apostolic church of Jesus Christ, who came "not to destroy men's lives, but to save them"? Do these bitter fruits prove the tree to be the blessed and true vine, outside of which is no Christianity?

If it be said that Protestants have also persecuted, there are two answers. First, when Protestants persecuted, it was done in opposition to their principles; and the logic of those principles soon put an end to the persecution. But when Catholics persecute, it is in accordance with their principles; and the logic of those principles continually tends to reproduce the persecution. Secondly, Protestants do not profess to be the only true Christians, and therefore are not expected to be so much better than the Catholics. But Catholics, because they claim a monopoly of Christianity, are bound to be free from all that is inconsistent with its principles.

Another fruit of true Christianity is social progress,

and an advance in national life. Roman Catholics then, if their assumption is correct, ought to be manifestly far in advance of Protestant countries in science, art, literature; in comfort, wealth, population, longevity; in good government, in the administration of justice, in the reform of criminals and vicious persons; in general education; in charitable institutions; in private morality, purity of manners, peaceful homes, general goodness. Now, if we compare Catholic nations with Protestant, do we find the former thus preeminent? Are Spain, Austria, Italy, Portugal, where the Catholic Church has ruled with absolute authority until the present time, so very much superior to Protestant Switzerland, Holland, Prussia, England, that he who runs can read their vast advantage? On the contrary, has not the result of this long Catholic teaching been in Italy, Spain, and Austria, a revolt against the church itself, often accompanied with a hatred of all religion?

Here are a few statistics of education: * The city of Turin, in 1848, while Catholic, spent 43,762 francs on education. It now spends one million. In 1860, under the good Catholic Bourbons, Naples had only 42 schools, and 3,000 pupils. Now it has 111 schools, and 17,000 pupils. All the Italian governments together, before 1860, spent only 8,000,000 francs. Now they spend 40,000,000. In

* See Contemporary Review, 1869, page 391.

1865, Italy, which had always been taught by the ecclesiastics, contained, out of every 100 men, 72 who could not read nor write, — and out of every 100 women, 84 who could not read nor write. In Protestant and Catholic Europe, out of every 10,000 persons, there are in the schools, — in Prussia, 1,520; in England, 1,400; in Holland, 1,280; in France, 1,660; in Belgium, 1,440; in Austria, 830; in Spain, 620; in Italy, 500; and in Russia, 150. Are the countries under Roman-Catholic influence as immeasurably superior to Protestant nations, in point of education, as the Roman theory requires? And shall we, in the United States, give up our unsectarian system of education, and adopt the sectarian system of the Catholic Church? This is what it asks us to do. It demands of us to change the grand system of free schools, the best institution of the state, in order to gratify the tastes of foreign priests, and emigrants from Europe. We receive them to our country; we make them citizens; many of them come as paupers, and in a few years become prosperous under our institutions. Then they ask us to give up our American system of universal education, which puts one in five out of our whole population into the schools, and take that of Italy which educates one out of twenty. But the American people have been at school too long to be deceived by the arguments of Mr. Hecker and his Jesuit friends.

As, according to Scripture, the meek are to inherit the earth; and as, according to Romanism, only the

Catholics can possess Christian meekness, it follows necessarily that the Catholic nations should far surpass the Protestant nations in all outward prosperity. They ought to be the wealthiest, strongest, best governed. In them alone, there ought to be the union of order and freedom, respect for law, and individual liberty. When the Reformation came, the Catholic writers predicted that it would end in anarchy and ruin, that every Protestant nation would be brought to utter destruction. For example, says a writer in the "Revue des Deux Mondes" (Jan. 15, 1870), —

"Bossuet, saluting with an eloquent voice the court of the widow of Charles I., believed himself able to enter into the counsels of the most high, in predicting that England was doomed to eternal wars, and that there was no possible remedy for her evils except in returning to her ancient faith and obedience. This prophecy was uttered by Bossuet twenty years before the final banishment of the Stuarts, which has given to this reprobate nation the longest period of power, peace, and freedom, ever enjoyed by any people of the world."

It is a favorite argument with our Roman-Catholic friends that Protestantism tends to infidelity and atheism. We must choose, they say, between Rome and utter infidelity.

A very careful, and apparently a very well-informed, writer in the "London Spectator" (June 20, 1869) takes a very different view of the situation. We quote a few passages: —

"One of the most marked signs of the times in Catholic countries is the extent to which irreligion is becoming a religion, a fanaticism as fierce and as propagandist as that of any creed has ever been. The change is not so perceptible in the Protestant States, where irreligion tends towards indifferentism, or rather to a tone of mind lower even than that. This, however, is not the tone of irreligion in the Catholic countries of the Continent. There the new attitude of Catholicism, its fiercely aggressive obscurantist and persecuting tone, has irritated scepticism to passion, to a hatred of Catholicism and its ministers, which in its ferocity and the concreteness of its manifestations recalls the days of the first French revolution. The laughing scepticism of 'polite society' is vanishing away, and in its place we have a propagandist spirit which cannot be content without overt acts.

"Men write, it is reported, from all parts of France to congratulate M. de Sainte-Beuve, most brilliant among essayists and among the few remaining masters of the lost art of conversation, to congratulate him on maintaining the 'sacred cause' of materialism in the Senate; and one such correspondent signs himself a member 'of the grand diocese,' thus making of denial not only a creed, but an ecclesiastical organization. Others, said to be thousands in number, bind themselves by oath never to accept the services of the Church in life, in death, or after death; to be married by civil ceremonial, to reject the 'last offices,'—which in Catholic countries have a social as well as religious importance,—and to be buried in unconsecrated ground. Our readers remember the astounding explosion of materialism among the students from all parts of the world who assembled at Liége to advertise their scorn and hatred of the ideas involved in the words 'God,' and 'soul,' and 'revelation,' and 'church,' a scorn and hate to which words seemed inadequate to give expression except in phrases that smelt of blood.

"In Belgium, where Ultramontanism has selected its battle-ground, materialism, utter and propagandist, is the creed of all but the religious, and is accompanied by a desire not merely to quit, but to put down the church as an evil thing, a foe to human society. The struggle is regarded as one between civilization and the Syllabus, as a warfare between irreconcilable ideas, in which every weapon is to be welcomed and quarter is disgraceful. M. de Montalembert, who, if a bigot, is furthest of mankind from a fool, declares publicly his belief that Paganism is winning, that the Continent is on the eve of a burst of irreligion, or hatred to religion, such as even the Revolution did not produce, in which all institutions claiming to be divine will be overthrown, and men commence the organization of a new and secularist world.

"That revolt of the schoolmasters in Austria was a revolt of the leaders of the peasantry, and was directed against ideas as well as against priests. It is stated that the Kaiser has admitted to the Vatican that on religious matters he is not a free agent; that all his soldiers could not enable him to veto the 'Godless bills;' and whether this account is correct or not, it is certain that the Austrian masses never got so excited on any secular matter. We have often reminded our readers of the fact that a city riot in Belgium always includes an attack on priests or monasteries; and the curious state of affairs in the department of Charente is a present illustration of the state of feeling. The priests there are being protected by Lancers from the hands of their flocks, who, were the soldiers withdrawn, would tear them in pieces. The very best friends the clerical order can have are the few highly intellectual men who strive to reconcile Rome with the modern world, who maintain that Christianity is compatible with any form of material civilization. To such men, the only men who stand between them and the materialists, and the only teachers who might in the last resort teach the masses that no dogma can produce hunger, that freedom is consistent with belief in the real presence, and that the unity of the church does not increase the conscription, the Ultramontanes, constrained by Rome, impelled by fear for themselves, driven by terror for the future of mankind, offer the Syllabus, under penalty of being considered foes like the Voltairians and the materialists. Naturally, the intellectual Catholics and the laity refuse, being unable to deny what they see, — that civilization is good; and the church is really reduced to what its enemies call it, a corporation hostile to society, and as such, in the judgment of those enemies, to be *écrasée*, razed off the ground it cumbers. The church offers in Catholic Europe only the alternatives of abject obedience or hostility; and Europe, unable to obey, without discretion accepts the alternative. It is not with pleasure, but with pain, that we record a growing doubt whether M. de Montalembert is not in the right; whether, if Rome does not change her policy, Europe may not see an explosion of irreligion, or fanatical hatred to religion of every kind, false and true alike, which will make the last quarter of this century the darkest through which modern man has passed. We like not Catholicism, with its sacerdotal claims, or Ultramontanism, with its machine-like obedience; but either is better, Hindooism is better, we had almost written Fetichism is better, than the foul creed which papal madness is establishing, — the creed which has for its solitary profession the dogma, 'Sugar is sweet.'"

Some Catholic controversialists remind us that a great many Protestants in New England have gone from orthodox Protestantism to Unitarianism and Universalism, and that many have gone from these to transcendentalism, rationalism, radicalism; and, for aught I know, some have gone on from these to atheism.

But this does not prove that Protestantism is logically bound to go on to Unitarianism, Universalism, radicalism, and atheism. It does not prove that there is no logical stand-point between Romanism and atheism. For, suppose we admit that, as a matter of fact and history, atheism comes out of radicalism, radicalism out of Unitarianism, and Unitarianism out of Protestantism; where did Protestantism, as a matter of fact, come from? Did it not come out of Romanism? Martin Luther and all the original Protestants were Catholics before they became Protestants. If, therefore, you say that because atheism comes out of Protestantism, therefore Protestantism is the mother of atheism; then Catholicism is the grandmother of atheism, for Protestantism came from it.

I grant that the tendency which takes men from Romanism to Protestantism is the same tendency that afterwards takes them on to rationalism and atheism. It is the tendency to free thought. It is the tendency to throw off human authority and to think for one's self. Out of that tendency came Protestantism; out of that tendency, carried to an extreme, comes atheism. But who says that logic requires us to carry a principle to extremes? How does it appear that it is reasonable to rush from one extreme to the opposite?

Catholics believe that there is a tendency in Protestantism toward rationalism and atheism, and conclude from that, without proving it, that this is a logical and rational tendency. But we do not reason so in other things. We usually suppose that the reasonable view is between two extremes. Horace says, "While fools shun one extreme, they run into another."

The tendency of a cautious man is to be too cautious, that is, timid; the tendency of courage is toward rashness; the tendency of self-respect is to pride; the tendency of humility is to diffidence. But we do not usually say that, therefore, there is no rational and logical ground between rashness and cowardice, between pride and diffidence. Then why should we say that if we believe in God and Christ, we must also logically believe in the Roman Church and all its assumptions? Is there no medium between atheism and superstition, between bigotry and scepticism? When in all other things we consider it irrational to go from one extreme to another, why consider it rational in religion? Protestantism is the true medium between Romanism, which submits reason to authority, and that ultra-rationalism which, like the spider, spins its whole web out of its own bowels.

But, in truth, Protestantism, instead of helping the tendency of free thought toward atheism, hinders it: it keeps men from atheism, instead of sending them forward into it. In Roman-Catholic countries, as soon as a man begins to doubt the infallibility of the church, he goes right on into atheism. In Protestant countries, when a Roman-Catholic doubts, he becomes a Protestant, a Unitarian, or at worst a deist. The greatest outbreak of atheism, in modern times, was in France, shortly before the French Revolution. Now the Protestants had been extirpated by Louis XIV.; the Huguenots were driven out of France, and it was left purely Catholic. Yet in two generations nearly the whole intellect of the country had gone over into atheism. Dr. Priestley, being in Paris, shortly before the French Revolution, in the company of some *savans*, said he did not believe there was one real atheist in the world. "Count us," replied one of the Frenchmen: "every one here, except yourself, is an atheist." Almost the only men of eminence, not atheists, were Voltaire and Rousseau. Rousseau was brought up as a Protestant in Geneva: Voltaire was a great student of English Protestant writers, like Locke and Newton. As soon as free thought breaks out in the Catholic Church, it goes directly into atheism. There is no stopping-place. Blanco White testifies the same about Spain; and Protestantism had been rooted out of Spain by the inquisition. The same thing is true in Italy. Protestantism is the safety-valve for free thought. The Roman Church fastens it down, and the result is an explosion.

But, suppose that doubt does not come out, is the man or nation any better for that? The policy of the Roman Church is to repress all outbreaks of heresy: the policy of Protestant countries is to let them come out. That is why you often see and hear more of scepticism in Protestant countries than in Catholic.

Let it be understood that we are now not opposing Catholicism as a religion, but only its extravagant assumptions. If it were contented to take its place as one denomination, one expression of Christianity, we should not be called on to oppose it. But it is because it arrogantly claims to possess all of Christianity, and therefore becomes an exclusive and persecuting church, that we are bound, in the interest of Christian liberty, to oppose its pretensions, and to show their emptiness.

The day will come, let us hope, when these pretensions will be laid aside. When, in the providence of God, national churches are established everywhere independent of Rome, we may see the end of papal assumption. Then every church will admit itself to be an organ, and only one, in Christ's body; each co-operating with the rest for the good of all.

FOURTH STEP.

FROM THE LETTER TO THE SPIRIT.

"Τὸ πνεῦμά ἐστι τὸ ζωοποιοῦν,
ἡ σὰρξ οὐκ ὠφελεῖ οὐδέν."

John vi. 63.

"Οὗ δὲ τὸ πνεῦμα κυρίου, ἐκεῖ ἐλευθερία."

2 Cor. iii. 17.

CHAPTER I.

Theology and Religion.

IN this last and briefer division of our little work, we shall treat of the future of Christianity. We have seen that Protestant Christianity is an advance on Romanism. But it does not follow from this that a poor Protestant is better than a good Catholic, nor that there is nothing good in the Church of Rome which Protestants do not possess. In truth, each church might learn something from the other; for each has advantages which the other needs, and deficiencies which the other might supply.

The Reformation was a providential event, came when it was needed, and has done an immense good to the world. Still, it has done some harm. It destroyed the outward church unity previously existing, and has not yet substituted a better kind. Each church has taken to itself a part of the Christian life, and is wanting in another part. Rome has more of order, system, organization, unity; the Protestant Church, more of freedom, variety, activity, and progress. In Romanism there is more of sentiment, more of worship, more of the womanly and affectionate side of life. In Protestantism there is more of conscience, of truthfulness, of intellectual activity, more of the manly side of life. Each needs what the other has; and the church of the future must unite the advantages of both.

But this reconciliation can only be effected by going down deeper, and going up higher, in the Christian life. We must forget the things behind, and reach out to those before. We must pass from the letter of Christianity to its spirit. And the first step is to comprehend the difference between theology and religion.

So long as these two are identified, sectarianism and bigotry will continue to divide the church. If I believe that the soul is saved by truth, as the Scripture asserts, and then confound truth in the soul with the form in which it is expressed, I shall consider my particular form of truth essential to salvation. Then I cannot, and ought not, to tolerate any variety. "Truth is one," I say. "If I am right, you are wrong, and *vice versâ*." It is therefore essential to Christian progress to see that the letter of truth is one thing, and the spirit of truth something very different; in other words, to see the difference between theology and religion.

What then is religion?

Religion is looking up, with reverence, love, and homage to the Invisible Perfection, — not in us, but above us. When I see the honest and faithful dog, looking up with devoted affection to the mysterious mind of man, there is a certain rudimental religion in that loving gaze; more so, I think, than in any mere effort at self-improvement or self-culture. Religion lifts us above ourselves in the admiration of something better and higher. If the God I worship is not as good as I am; if I think him more powerful, but unjust, vindictive, cruel, — then this is not religion, but superstition. It does not lift me up, but drags me down. When we find in ourselves something higher than ourselves, — purer, nobler, better, — we then are listening to God's voice in the soul. We are tempted, we go astray, we often do wrong; but there is a voice within, a voice of eternal right, speaking in the conscience, which never consents to our wrong. It is something higher than we are; it is God speaking to us as the eternal right.

We are often poor, mean, low, but there is in the soul an ideal of something better than we. In the midst of our folly and fault, there stands before us the pure image of serene goodness, and we cannot but reverence it. This also is God, showing himself to the soul; and when we catch a glimpse of this infinite beauty, purity, holiness, — not in us, but above us, — we have a sense of religion. When we look constantly, steadily, deliberately at this image of perfect goodness, we become religious. The sight and worship of this supreme excellence is religion. Putting it into words, and defining it in propositions, is theology.

There are hours in which I catch in nature the sense

of a universal presence; above nature, yet in it. In the infinite beauty of a summer day; in the solemn majesty of a winter night; in the sublimity of ocean lashed by the tempest into black roaring waves, over whose slippery sides the vessel staggers and reels through the pitiless storm; in the deep stillness of autumn woods, where no sound comes but the dropping of nuts or the faint whistle of the lonely bird,— amid all these scenes there comes up in the soul the sense of a great unity, a substance below all, a power above all, a life within all; and we come face to face with God. This is religion. Analyzing this sentiment, and stating it in metaphysical formulas, is theology.

When I open the Gospels, and read the words of Jesus, I find myself in sunshine. Light and warmth are united in his teachings, inseparably. The light warms, the warmth illuminates. He makes goodness lovely, natural, simple, easy. He is no austere moralist, no cold lawgiver, but a man among men; not bound by the etiquette of religious ceremonies, but just as willing to take a walk with his disciples on the Sabbath as on any other day. He does not use the stereotyped language of piety; but he teaches by the dough in the bread-trough, by the door through which he passes, by the net his disciples are pulling out of the water, with good and bad fish sticking in its meshes. He makes God seem near, and heaven close by, and life full of good opportunity, and every soul capable of goodness. He is my friend, my teacher, my brother; and his thought seems to become a part of mine. That is religion. Then some learned man comes and defines Jesus; saying how much of him is human, and how much divine; and shows me how it is proper to talk of him according to the metaphysics of Aristotle. That is theology.

Perhaps I have never prayed; or I have *said* my prayers, repeating by rote some formula. God has seemed a great way off, and very high up, and I do not know whether he hears me or not. If I speak to him, I think it proper to praise and adore him very much, using the grandest words I can find. But some day, in my hour of need, — in my great sorrow, when the darling of my heart lies cold by my side; when my love is deceived; when all my hopes are shattered, — I suddenly find myself talking with my God, as though he indeed were close by, and could help me into his peace. In a moment, every thing in my heart is changed. "He has rebuked the winds and waves, and there is a great calm." After that I know what prayer means. After that I go to God just as I am, — poor, weak, sinful, — and talk with him as a friend. After that, whenever I feel too weak for my work, I just look up, inwardly; and I find myself fed with the daily bread I needed. This is religion. But when I take these experiences, classify them, philosophize about them, and state them as an article of faith, that is theology.

If I have this threefold experience of God; if I find him in nature and providence as a universal Father, taking care of all his children, sending sun and rain on the evil and the good alike; if I find him as taught by Christ, and shown in his life, as the friend of my soul; if I find him also in my heart in prayer, giving me light and peace, — how does it help me to be told that this is a trinity, and that God is three persons in one substance? Such a statement may or may not suit my intellect; but how does it help my heart?

Religion belongs to the heart; it is love. Theology belongs to the head; it is speculation. But love is one and the same thing always, while speculation is always different. Love is always one. A mother's love for her little child is the same, whether she is a queen in Buckingham palace, or a beggar nursing her baby under a hedge. A gentleman told me that he went to church in the Isle of Wight, where Queen Victoria was also worshipping. After church he stood to see her come out with her husband and babies; and reported her as saying, "Shall we go home, Albert, or shall we take the children to drive?" It did not seem a very memorable speech to bring back to America; but he remembered it, because it showed him that a queen was just like any other mother after all. That is why we all are thrilled with poetry; for poetry speaks the language of the heart. When the baby in Homer cries because his father has his helmet on, and Hector takes it off in order to kiss his child, — that touch of nature overleaps the twenty-five centuries between, and makes Hector and ourselves akin. But when the metaphysician explains the theory of paternal love, and shows us its theology, we feel that we are several thousand years apart. Religion, which is love, is always one and the same; theology differs with every different thinker. Is it not curious, then, that Christians should have always endeavored to unite the church by theology, instead of by religion? It is as though we should try to tie the rivers together with ropes made of sand, instead of letting them flow together in the ocean.

Religion, wherever you find it, as far as it goes, is always one and the same thing. It is always reverence, faith, obedience, gratitude, hope, and love. Father Huc, the Roman Catholic, found a religion like his own among the Buddhist monks in the Lamasery of Thibet. Bishop Southgate found a piety like his own in the aged Mohammedan, bowing his head to the ground in prayer to Allah. I knew a man who thought that no Unitarian could be a Christian; but who was converted from that infidelity, merely by opening a chamber-door unexpectedly, and finding his Unitarian friend on his knees before God. It has happened that men, in the bitterness and rage of sectarian cruelty, have dragged their theological opponent to the stake; but that when they have seen him calm amid the flames, calling on God, they have rushed away in despair, crying, "We are damned for ever:

we have burnt a saint." Religion, a sentiment, created by the Spirit of God in human hearts, is one and the same; while theology differs, with every age, with every church, with every man.

But, it may be said, "Is there then no truth which is equally true for all times and all men?" For example, is it not always true, and the same truth, to say, "There is one God, the Father?" And is not that a theological statement, a proposition for the intellect, the article of a creed?

I answer that the statement, "There is one God," does not mean exactly the same thing in the mouth of a Unitarian, and in the mouth of a Trinitarian. The Unitarian means by it a simple unity; the Trinitarian, a complex unity. And when I say, "God is a Father;" does that mean the same to him who has been brought up by a kind and tender father, and to him who never had a father, or had a brutal and vicious one? The child who has had a bad father, and a good mother, would understand the truth better by hearing, "God is my mother." Therefore no theological statement, even in the simplest form, means the same thing to all minds. But filial love, in a child's heart, so far as it is real, is always the same. If it exist at all, and so far as it exists, it is the same thing. There may be more or less of it, but the radical feeling is one.

The Apostle Paul, I think, taught exactly what I have been saying, when he declared that knowledge, even his own knowledge and teaching about God, was partial, imperfect, and would come to an end; while faith, hope, and love would never come to an end. "We know in part, and we prophesy (or teach) in part," says he; "but when that which is perfect is come, then that which is in part shall be done away." Modern philosophy teaches the same, in calling all knowledge relative; made up of the sight of the thing itself, and the capacity of the one who sees it. The form of knowledge, which is the verbal statement, changes and passes; but the substance of knowledge, which is the inward experience in the soul, remains. Knowledge passes; truth remains. There are, most certainly,

"Truths which wake
To perish never," —

truths, hidden in the heart, concerning God, duty, immortality, love, and peace.

The question we are discussing, it will be observed, is not whether right opinions are not desirable, useful, and important, but whether they are essential. Can a man be a true Christian whose opinions about Christianity are all wrong? That is the point. Now, since we find good men holding all varieties of opinion, it is evident that goodness does not depend on sound opinion. There is no sect so small, so poor, so heretical, as not to have its saints, its heroes, its martyrs. When the Quakers came to New England as a new sect, no wonder our Puritan Fathers thought it impossible that they could be Christians. The Quakers began by rejecting the whole Calvinistic theology, — the trinity, the atonement, and total depravity. Then they declared that the Bible was not the only rule, nor the highest rule, of Christian faith and practice ; but that the Holy Spirit was above the Bible. Then they flatly contradicted the fundamental article of all New-England theology, — that man was unable, until he was converted, to think or feel or act rightly. On the contrary, they declared that there is in all men an inner light, — a "light which lightens every man who comes into the world," a "grace of God, bringing salvation, which has appeared to all men," and that every man who heard that voice in his soul might find the way to heaven. Going further, they rejected baptism and the Lord's Supper, and also the Christian ministry. And so, having renounced all orthodox theology, they ended by disowning the existing church, and all ecclesiastical institutions, as the work of Satan. Then they proceeded further still, and took up the foundations of civil society, — refused to take oaths, pay taxes, serve on juries, do military service, or hold slaves. And to make themselves still more unpopular with the common people, — which resents mostly any innovation in external matters, — they dressed queerly, they talked queerly, and they lived queerly. No wonder that our Puritan Fathers were shocked, and tried to keep them from coming into New England. And it is no wonder, though it is a thing to be for ever lamented, that when they could not keep them from coming here, — in those days when every one persecuted, and thought persecution the right thing, — they should have hung them on Boston Common. And yet, to-day, who questions or denies the Christianity of the Friends? Who denies that they have just as much religion, to say the least, as any other communion?

In one sense, all right doctrines are essential to Christianity; that is, all are essential to its integrity as a system of thought. So every organ, limb, and fibre is essential to the integrity of the human body. The hairs on the head, the nails on the fingers, are essential to make a complete human being. A bald man, a deaf man, a one-legged man is not wholly a man. But a near-sighted man, or a man who has lost his arm, can live. In theology, every doctrine is essential to the integrity of the system. But no one, now, considers the imputation of Adam's sin, or even election and reprobation to be essential doctrines. Yet Lutherans and Calvinists used to fight more savagely and bitterly over these questions than any would do now about the trinity. Logically, no part of a theological system is unessential. Every doctrine, down to the most minute, is necessary to the integrity of the whole. It is idle, therefore, to select two or three, and say that these are essential, and that those, and only those, are Christians who believe in them. One thing or the other, Make the tree good, and all its fruit good; or else make the tree corrupt, and all its fruit corrupt: for the tree is known by its fruit.

That the tree is known by its fruit is a fundamental Christian axiom; but neither bigotry nor sectarianism can accept it. They do not judge the tree by the fruit, but the fruit by the tree. In the famous convention in 1869, held at Portland, of the different branches of the Young Men's Christian Association, it was laid down that all evangelical Christians might be members. Some one asked, "Who are evangelical Christians?" and some one else answered, "Those who love the Lord Jesus in sincerity." Then an honest man from Fall River said there were Unitarians in his town who loved the Lord Jesus as much as anybody else: were they evangelical? To which a learned divine from Pittsburg or Wheeling replied that a Unitarian *could* not love Jesus: it was impossible. So he judged the fruit by the tree. The tree is labelled a Unitarian tree; then it cannot bring forth good fruit. The fruit looks good, smells good, tastes good; it looks like love for Jesus; it seems like honesty, piety, submission, penitence, faith. But it comes from a Unitarian tree; therefore throw it away, it is all bad. But if we cannot know goodness when we see it, all the foundations of belief crumble. How can Christianity be proved to be true, unless we know what goodness is before we become Christians? We argue that Christianity is a religion favorable to human virtue; that it makes men better; that Jesus himself was pure, holy, and good beyond all precedent. But all this argument gives way, if we are unable to tell a good man, until we learn what creed he holds.

It is on this fundamental distinction, between religious experience which gives us a knowledge of God, Christ, and Christianity, and theological speculation which gives us only opinions about them, that the battle of Christian freedom and Christian union is to be fought and won. It is the only solid foundation for either. So long as men believe Christianity to be a matter of opinion, they will feel bound to be exclusive, to separate, to persecute, to enslave their own minds and those of others. Liberal Christians in all sects are therefore fighting the battle of humanity and Christianity. They contend for that knowledge of God and Christ of which Jesus speaks when he says, "Flesh and blood have not revealed it unto thee, Peter, but my Father in heaven." No doctrine is essential which man can teach man, which flesh and blood can reveal, which can be packed into propositions, put into logical boxes, and carried about by tract societies. All essential knowledge is born of life, and is the faith of the heart. "With the heart man believeth unto righteousness." Paul does not pray that Christ may dwell in the heads of the Ephesians, but in their hearts.

Religion is the root of theology, not theology the root of religion. The life is the light of man, not the reverse. Filling the brain with doctrines about God and Christ, before life has led the soul to see them, often tends to benumb the spiritual nature rather than to quicken it. Instead of teaching young persons doctrines and speculations about Jesus, lead them to Jesus himself. Let them read his words, study his life, and apply it daily in their own. We can never know God by speculation: we know him as we live from him and to him, as we endeavor to serve him, as we come near him in practical obedience, as we love and help his children.

This distinction also is the guarantee of perfect intellectual freedom. So long as we think that any form of opinion, any method of statement, may be essential to salvation, we cannot examine it freely. We are held by our hopes and our fears to certain conclusions, before we begin to inquire. We are working in chains. Let us admit and believe that a man may, in his speculations, be even an atheist, and if he is honest, yet really be a Christian in his heart. Let us believe that many a man who is all wrong in his theology may be all right in his faith. Let it be seen that love alone abides, — love, rooted in faith, made strong by hope. Then we become free to inquire, modestly but faithfully, into all truth.

And this principle alone will produce union in the church, and so enable it to convert the world to Christ and God. Jesus in his last prayer intimates that the world cannot be converted to him till his disciples are one: "That they all may be one; as thou, Father, art in me, and I in thee, that they may also be one in us; that the world may believe that thou hast sent me." As long as Christians consent to unite only with those who agree with them in intellectual results, so long the church will never become one. But if they will unite with all honest men who are seeking to know God and Christ and to do right, then there is a chance of their finally coming all to agree in opinion. But the only real unity, the only unity which Christianity demands, is THE UNITY OF THE SPIRIT IN THE BOND OF PEACE.

I lately saw a picture of Christ among the doctors. The little child was sitting in the midst, and with childlike ardor was reaching out his hands while he uttered his thoughts about God and truth. The old doctors were standing and sitting around; some searching their books to find an answer to his questions; some asking each other what they thought about it; some repeating, evidently from their memory, what they had learned before. They represented the orthodox tradition; he, the immediate revelation. They stood for sound, safe, conservative theology; he, for that divine religion which makes all things new in the heart, the life, and the world.

CHAPTER II.

THE CREED OF CHRISTENDOM.

THE object of this chapter is to show what are the essential unities of belief in the Christian Church. I shall endeavor to present the creed of Christendom, the faith of the true Catholic Church; and to show how many more, and more important, are the convictions in which Christians unite, than those about which they separate and divide.

It is true that when we first look at the church, it seems a mere battle-field of warring creeds and opposing sects. Sectarianism began very early among Christians, as far back as the days of the apostles and the church of Corinth. Some were Paulists, some were Apollosians, some Peterites, and some Christians, with an emphasis on the first syllable, so as to make even that name of union a sign of division. In a century or two Christians were murdering each other in the streets of Alexandria, about the difference beween ὁμοούσιος and ὁμοιούσιος. In the tenth century the eastern and western churches divided on the question whether the Holy Spirit proceeded from the Father, or from the Father and the Son. Afterwards came the crusades against heretics, and the furies of the inquisition; and later still the horrible wars of religion, laying waste half of Europe. This now seems to us like a hideous dream. At present we only persecute each other by calling names; and even that luxury seems fast disappearing. To be a misbeliever formerly was to be a miscreant; now it is rather an honor. Men whom no one would take the pains of listening to, if they preached the old-fashioned doctrines, have a considerable following if they are supposed to be the founders of a new religion, or the denouncers of the ancient faith.

The bitterness of old sectarian bigotry has very much departed, but separation often exists where there is no hostility. We have almost done fighting with each other about our differences of opinion, but as yet there is no union. Union will come only when we perceive the fact that we really are at one in all essentials. At present we only tolerate each other, and stand apart. But when we realize that we agree in one hundred points where we differ in one; that we agree in all essentials, and only differ in unessentials; that the practical working faith of all Christians is about the same, then we shall be really willing to co-operate, to unite, and to love each other. It is for this reason that I shall now devote myself to showing in how many things Christians are all agreed.

The first article in the creed of Christendom is this:

"We believe in God, the Father Almighty, Maker of heaven and earth." Christians dispute in regard to the metaphysical nature of the Deity, as to the mystery of the Trinity and the hypostatic union. Some say that there is a threefold personality — or a threefold mode of being, or a threefold somewhat — in the Deity; and others contend that there is not. But so obscure and difficult is this question, that it is almost impossible for the most acute theologian to express himself intelligibly concerning it, and it is quite impossible to find any Scripture terms in which to state it; and so it resolves itself at last into a question of words, — not, What ought we to believe? but, What ought we to say? Meantime, all Christians believe God to be one, in every practical sense. We do not worship a pantheon of Gods, as did the Greeks and heathen: we worship one Supreme Being, — above all, through all, and in us all. All Christians agree, as against atheism, that there is a God; all agree, as against polytheism, that there is but one God; all agree, as against materialism, that he is a Spirit; all agree, as against pantheism, that he is a person; all agree, as against superstition, that he is infinitely good, not a God of wrath, but of love; and all agree, as against enthusiasm and fanaticism, that he requires a reasonable and a moral service, not one of madness or folly. No doubt all kinds of aberrations have come into Christianity; there has been in it pantheism and polytheism, materialism and superstition, enthusiasm and fanaticism. But none of them has been accepted into the creed of Christendom, all have been condemned by its unanimous verdict. The doctrine of the universal church has been, that there is but one God, the Father Almighty, Maker of heaven and earth; that he is a Spirit; that he is one; that he is a person; that he is love, and dwells in love; and that he asks for a manly, free, and reasonable service.

The second article in the creed of Christendom is this: "We believe in Jesus as the Christ, the Son of God."

Christians dispute about the nature and rank of Christ in the creation. Was he God? Was he man? Was he some great archangel, above man, below God? But those who call him God can only explain this Deity by speaking of a mysterious union between the Infinite Spirit and the human soul of Christ. And those who call him man must also admit that he was intimately united with God in thought, heart, and will. Even the most radical Christians do not call him a common man, but a very uncommon man. Who, that claims to be a Christian at all, doubts or questions the purity, the truth, the humility, the courage, the human sympathy of Jesus? Who denies that the truth he taught has been for the healing of the nations? Who can resist the conviction that the movement originated by him is the greatest fact in human history? All Christians are agreed here, — that he taught love to God, and love to man, as the supreme law; and that higher than this no one can go.

When we assert with all of Christendom, that Jesus is the Christ, the Son of God, what do we mean? We mean that his method of overcoming evil with good is to conquer the sin and misery of the world. We mean that his truth is at last to convince all understandings, that his love is to win all hearts, and that to his divine holiness every knee is to bow. So he is to be the Christ, the King of the world. He is our master, because he reveals to us a higher spiritual law than any other. He is our Saviour, because nothing saves us from evil and sin like the conviction he imparts of the infinite tenderness and universal fatherly love of God. And yet he is our brother, made in all respects like his brethren.

The third article in the creed of Christendom is the Bible.

All Christians believe in the Bible as the best of books, — better than any other, sacred or profane. They may differ about the way in which it was inspired. Some may think that the Holy Spirit played on the writers as a man plays on a flute; some may believe that every word and letter of the Bible is absolutely true. Others may believe the writers inspired as all men are inspired, only more so; and may deny that inspiration is infallibility. But all Christians see in the Bible a book full of God, and full of truth. It is sweetness and strength. It is comfort in sorrow; it is guidance in duty; it lifts us near to God; it purifies the soul. When we go to sit by the bedside of the sick and dying, what words like these will lift the heart to a sight of invisible eternal realities? What preparation for the dangers of life, better than a knowledge of these writings? It is a profitable book, — all admit that, — profitable for doctrine, discipline, and instruction in righteousness. All the churches believe in the Bible.

The fourth article in the creed of Christendom is the Holy Spirit.

"I believe in the Holy Ghost." Is there any Christian who does not believe in the Holy Ghost? Christians differ as to whether it is a person in the Trinity, and as to whether its influences are irresistible or persuasive. Some think it comes and goes; others, that it is God with us always, ready to send love and truth into the heart which is open to receive it. Some think that it comes to put something in us which was not there before; others, that it is like the influence of one soul on another. I talk with my friend. I am angry. I am unhappy. I am in a bad, wicked mood of mind. But my friend is calm, strong, just, gentle, generous. As I talk with him, somehow my bad passion melts away, my evil purpose dies out of me. It is not his argument which has convinced me; he has used none. It is his Holy Spirit which has convinced me; that I could not resist. So God's Holy Spirit convinces us when we put ourselves in communion with him.

What should we be if we could not feel that ineffable presence? How desperate our life, if we did not know that the infinite love is always waiting to bless us. As a man closes the curtains of his chamber, and shuts out the day, so we often close our heart against God, because we are determined on some course which we know to be wrong. But as, when we open the shutters, and draw the curtains, the light streams in; so whenever we are willing to turn our souls to God, his light is ready to illuminate us. We all believe in the Holy Spirit, — the Spirit which leads us into new truth; which enables Christianity to make progress; which receives more light from the greater experience of the church and the soul; the Spirit which dwelleth with us, and shall be in us. The creed of Christendom declares, "I believe in the Holy Spirit."

The creed of Christendom has also included a belief in the church.

Christians have contended and fought as to which was the true church, but all have believed in some church. All believe in the communion of saints, — in the brotherhood of those who hold the same truth, serve the same Master, seek the same heaven. The essence of a church is where two or three meet together in the name of Christ. Two or three men, with a strong belief in any thing, make a church. Their belief draws them together and keeps them in sympathy. We have churches in politics, — the Democratic Church and the Republican Church. We have churches in reforms, — the Anti-Slavery Church and the Temperance Church.

We have churches in society, — Aristocratic and Plebeian. We have Conservative clubs, Union clubs, and Woman's-Rights clubs. Ideas organize associations; the largest, deepest, highest ideas organize the largest and most enduring associations. A church, in some form, is a need of human nature.

There are those who stay outside of churches, and prefer to spend their Sunday in reading, sleeping, or taking a walk. I think, however, that they lose a good deal. They excommunicate themselves from the blessed sense of human brotherhood. In other places, men meet with those related to themselves in some special ways, — meet their customers, meet their associates, meet those who belong to their clique. In the Church of Christ they meet all God's children in universal ways. Novalis said that Christianity was the last word of Democracy. Christianity alone unites us with all mankind. Those who think they have no need of the church, who think they have outgrown the church, are much mistaken. They grow small, narrow, puny, in their isolation from the great tide of human life, which only can flow together in the house of God, where all are one before Him, the Universal Father.

Therefore Christians agree in accepting the church as the brotherhood of believers.

And again: the creed of Christendom includes the same moral law, — the same conceptions of duty, right, honesty, purity, truth, generosity, patience, forbearance, forgiveness, temperance, sobriety, love to God, and love to man.

There has never been a denomination founded on any new ideas concerning right and wrong. There has never been any one which denounced another as infidel because it disbelieved the golden rule. There has never been any bitter theological controversy about the meaning of the sermon on the mount. No church has ever excommunicated its members for rejecting the ten commandments. Bigotry has always consisted in believing more than others, never in doing more than others. The creed of Christendom has always contained, as its essence, love to God and love to man.

The creed of Christendom also includes a belief in immortality and the future life.

What sect or party among Christians does not accept this and cling to it? They differ as to the circumstances of resurrection, judgment, heaven, and hell. Some insist that we shall rise again in the same material body; others that we shall rise in a spiritual body. Some think the judgment of Christ is to be in one place and at one time; others that it is a perpetual judgment, taking place now, and to take place more fully hereafter. Some believe heaven and hell divided by physical barriers, and each to be a sort of receptacle, a place into which souls are to be put. Others believe heaven to be the state of the soul, — a state of love, peace, and joy in God; and hell a state of the soul, — selfishness and falsehood and bitter hatred. But all believe in immortality, resurrection, heaven, and hell.

Again: there are different ways of believing in the

atonement of Jesus; but all Christians believe that Jesus has in some way brought the soul to God.

One view assumes that it was necessary that Christ should die, in order to produce an effect on God. He died to satisfy the wrath of God, or the holiness of God, or the justice of God, or the moral government of God. He died to reconcile two attributes in the divine nature; to enable God to be just, and merciful too. God wished to pardon, but could not do it because his justice required him to punish some one. Christ said, "Punish me, and pardon them." God did this, and so was able to pardon without violating any principle of justice. It was a supernatural transaction, something taking place in the transcendental world. This is one view of the atonement.

Another view is, that Christ died to reconcile man to God, not to reconcile God to man. He died to bring us to God, not to bring God to us. The effect of his death, as of his life, was wrought on the human soul. He came to make us see the infinite tenderness, the infinite pity, of our heavenly Father; to make us see that he cares for us more than we care for ourselves. He makes atonement, by making man and God one; by making the church one; by making nations, races, classes one; by doing away with war, tyranny, slavery, envy, jealousy, and all uncharitableness. It is no transaction in the supernatural world, but one which takes place here in time. Whenever two who were divided are reconciled by the gospel; whenever the proud become humble, and the lowly courageous, Jesus makes atonement. The atonement of Christ is universal reconciliation, proceeding from a revelation of God's love. That is the view of the atonement, according to some thinkers. But all Christians believe in the atoning, or unity-making power of Christ and his gospel.

Once more: there are different ways of regarding salvation by Christ, but all Christians believe in some Christian salvation.

One view considers salvation as the rescue of the soul from future suffering, from a future hell. Jesus has paid our debt: we can now be saved by believing in him. It is a future salvation. It is escape from future punishment. This is one view.

The other view regards punishment, in this world and the next, as the natural consequence of wrong-doing; as something fixed in the very laws of nature, something which cannot be avoided by any expedient, and something which it is good for us to endure. The object of punishment is to purify and improve. It takes place here, and will take place hereafter. There is no use in trying to escape it; it is inevitable. Salvation does not consist, therefore, in removing punishment. It is rescue from sin. Jesus saves us by giving us a new heart; teaching us to love what is good; putting a new life into us, by which we can rise above ourselves; bringing us into communion with God and heaven. He is not a future, but a present Saviour. He gives heaven here, the beginning of heaven hereafter. Whenever a man, woman, or child, makes a sacrifice for the sake of truth, he enters into heaven. Whenever we are able to trust God, and talk with him as a friend, we go into heaven. Whenever we love Jesus, and try to do his work in the world, and help his little ones, we are sitting in heavenly places with him. Jesus saves us by inspiring us with faith, hope, courage; by making us love our fellow-creatures, as God loves them. He saves us, not from any outward hell, but the hell of our own passions, our ungovernable desires, our cold hearts, our bitter jealousy, our folly, recklessness, insincerity. He saves us by giving us the love of truth, purity, goodness. This is the view of Christ's salvation, according to many Christians. But all Christians believe in some salvation through Christ.

Thus are we all baptized into the Father, the Son, and the Holy Ghost. The doctrine of the Trinity, which has been made a narrow, unintelligible, and exclusive formula, is one day, in a larger form, to be recognized as the most inclusive of all doctrines; the fullest statement of the length, breadth, depth, and height of the divine Pleroma, the fulness of him who filleth all in all. It will include the past, the present, and the future. When we say, "We believe in the Father," we include in that statement the declaration that whatever God has made is divine. The whole past is divine. There is a sacred meaning in all nature, science, history. God is in all that has ever been, from the foundation of the world. He has inspired all the prophets of all religions; he has fed the souls of his children in all lands and climes; he has disinherited none. He is the universal Father.

And when we truly say, "We believe in the Son," we shall accept every form of human nature as a part of the universal church of Christ. Jesus, as the Son, is to bring all men to his Father. Christ is to be the great atonement, leading all souls to God. Every human being is a son of God, all are loved by him; he wishes all to be saved, and to come to the knowledge of the truth. As God the Father is in nature and history, so through the Son he descends into humanity, and unites himself with mankind. None so poor, low, ignorant, as not to have a share in this redeeming love. God, who as the Creator and Father has been in all the past, as the Son is in the present life of mankind, is with us now and here; so that now is the accepted time, and now is the way of salvation.

And when we say that "we believe in the Holy Spirit," we announce the great hope for the future. All is to come right at last. Evil is to be overcome by good. Progress is the law of the universe, and progress will never end.

When Jesus first told his disciples of the coming of the Holy Ghost, it was in these words: —

"*I have many things to say unto you; but you cannot bear them now. But when that spirit of truth shall come, it shall lead you into all truth.*"

The Holy Spirit, therefore, comes to complete revelation. It fulfils what is in the four Gospels. It emancipates us from the letter of the New Testament, and carries out its divine spirit more fully. It makes Christianity not a stationary creed, but a progressive religion. It enables it to accept the valuable results of science, of heathen religion, and heathen philosophy, all that God has taught in other ways to his children. It makes Christianity an advancing religion, always abreast with the age; only a little before it, its leader and guide.

I cannot think that this dead formula of the Trinity is allowed to remain for nothing. I think it has a better meaning than those perhaps know who hold it. To me it means UNIVERSAL UNITY; Christianity showing us God in all things, — in nature, life, history, mankind, the present, and the future.

This view of Father, Son, and Spirit confounds and confutes all narrowness, — the narrowness of the science which rejects Christianity, and the narrowness of the Christianity which rejects science. It rebukes the narrowness of that sectarianism which rejects the universal church of human brotherhood; the narrowness of that conservatism which rejects every coming reform; and also the narrowness of reformers who reject and neglect the great history of the past.

We worship God the Father, through the Son, and in the Holy Spirit.

"One God, the Father of all, who is above all, and through all, and in us all."

"One Lord, Jesus Christ," who is the way, the truth, and the life. He is the door through which we enter on our upward way; the bread which feeds our life; the lamb slain from the foundation of the world; showing us how God comes to dwell among men, and to save all his children.

And "one Holy Spirit," the spirit of holiness, in which we walk, speak, live; which shows us better things to-day than we knew yesterday; which turns Christian belief into Christian experience; which makes us *live* Christianity, and not merely *talk it* or *think it*. One Holy Spirit, dwelling in the hearts of all good men and women and children, giving to them all, all the good they have.

Thus this formula teaches us that the same God who is above us is also the God who is with us, and the God who is in us. One God, whether seen in nature, or revelation, or life! One God, whether he came in the past, comes in the present, or is to come in the future!

When this view is realized, we shall have the true Communion of Saints, by which God shall unite all men in Christ, all men with each other, and all with himself.

Thus we see the unities of Christendom: we see how all Christians, no matter how much they differ, are essentially one. They differ because they are narrow; when they go deeper, and rise higher, they come together.

For they all believe in one God, one Christ, one Bible, one Law of Duty, one Church Universal, one Immortal Life, and one Holy Spirit.

Where they differ, it is because they know in part, and see in part; where they agree, it is because they supply the narrowness of their creed by the largeness of their love.

Cambridge: Press of John Wilson & Son.

www.ingramcontent.com/pod-product-compliance
Lightning Source LLC
LaVergne TN
LVHW020225110826
845151LV00003B/831

* 9 7 8 1 4 2 5 5 3 1 5 5 3 *